Sun Signs Made Simple

The Zodiac in a Nutshell

Jonathan Dee & Sasha Fenton

A Sterling / Zambezi Book

Sterling Publishing Co., Inc.

New York

Library of Congress Cataloging-in-Publication Data Available

2 4 6 8 10 9 7 5 3 1

Published in 2004 by
Sterling Publishing Co., Inc.
387 Park Avenue South
New York, NY 10016

Published and distributed in the UK soley by
Zambezi Publishing Limited
P.O. Box 221 Plymouth,
Devon PL2 2YJ (UK)

Distributed in Canada by Sterling Publishing
^{c}/o Canadian Manda Group
165 Dufferin Street
Toronto, Ontario, Canada M6K 3H6

Distributed in Australia by Capricorn Link (Australia) Pty Ltd.
P.O. Box 704, Windsor, NSW 2756, Australia

Typesetting by Zambezi Publishing, Plymouth UK

Sterling ISBN 1-4027-1491-2
Zambezi ISBN 1-903065-33-X

About the Authors

Jonathan Dee

They say that there are two sides to everybody, and in the case of Jonathan, the two sides are a deep interest in astrology and psychic subjects of all kinds on one side, and a love of history on the other.

Jonathan has been an astrologer, Tarot card reader, and psychic since the 1970s, having worked all over the UK and in the USA. He is well known on radio, television, and in a variety of magazines, both as a serious historian and folklorist in addition to his knowledge of astrology and allied subjects. He has written almost 100 books, covering a host of divinatory and spiritual subjects in addition to several historical ones. Jonathan has worked closely with Sasha Fenton on many successful writing, broadcasting, and lecturing projects.

In addition to his writing, Jonathan has been the regular daily astrologer for BBC Radio Wales for the past 18 years on a very popular Sony Broadcasting award-winning program. Whether speaking as an astrologer, Feng Shui expert, face reader, or a historian (ancient Egyptian history is his favorite), Jonathan always manages to fascinate his audience.

Jonathan lives in Cardiff, Wales, with a cute little mongrel called Tazmania.

Sasha Fenton

Sasha Fenton's dynamic career as a professional astrologer, palmist, and Tarot card reader began in 1974. She has now written over 120 books, mainly in the mind, body, and spirit genre, as well as on financial subjects. Her books have sold over 6.5 million copies, some with translations into ten different languages. Sasha now runs Zambezi Publishing with her husband, Jan Budkowski, but still indulges her passion for writing.

Best known for titles such as *Moon Signs, The Living Hand, How to Read your Star Signs, Fortune Telling by Tarot Cards,* and many years of the annual Astroguide Series co-authored with her close writing partner, Jonathan Dee, Sasha also wrote the stars column for *Woman's Own* magazine in Britain, and astrology and palmistry columns and numerous articles for major British magazines as well as many overseas publications. You can find out more about astrology, the mind, body, and spirit arena and Sasha by visiting her website at *www.sashafenton.com*

At present, Sasha has a regular live program on BBC Radio Devon, discussing a variety of psychic and spiritual subjects. She has been featured on most British radio and television stations, as well as stations in the USA, Australia, South Africa, and Bophuthatswana. *(Where's that? It's a South African homeland state...)*

Somehow, Sasha also managed to find time to serve as President of the British Astrological and Psychic Society (BAPS), Chair of the British Advisory Panel on Astrological Education, and on the Executive Council of the Writers' Guild of Great Britain.

Although her lecturing, broadcasting, and involvement with the world media are unlikely ever to stop, Sasha now enjoys spending more time on Zambezi Publishing with Jan, in the beautiful Devonshire countryside around Plymouth. She has two children and two granddaughters.

Contents

Introduction

Whether you only want to understand your own Sun sign or dazzle your friends by knowing so much about them, our book will give you the answer. It is full of bite-sized astrological insights. While we hope that you find our book fun to read, know that the information in it works because it is based on sound astrological insights.

You can discover the kind of house a typical Gemini would love to live in; the trees and plants associated with Taurus; or the countries ruled by Leo. You can check out why Aquarians are hard to fathom or whether Virgos and Capricorns really are careful with their money. You can gain valuable insight before jumping into a love affair with a fascinating Scorpio, or discover whether your Libra friend will give you the domestic harmony you crave. If you don't crave domestic harmony, how about considering an adventurous Sagittarian or a sexy Aries?

Naturally, you will want to check out your own Sun sign, but you won't be able to restrain yourself from also peering into the likes, dislikes, behavior (and some of the less attractive habits) of your friends and loved ones.

There are always variations among people of the same Sun sign, so we show you how to assess some of these as well by use of the Decan system. This demonstrates the variations among people born in different parts of each sign (i.e. early, middle, or late in the sign). Once you have established your Decan via our easy system, you can see why you differ from others who share your Sun sign. Later in this book, you will find charts that show those people with whom you are most compatible for love, friendship, and work, along with the signs with which you are unlikely to harmonize. Once again, you can check these not only for your Sun sign, but also for your Decan sign, thus producing more accuracy.

Finally, our book even shows you the best times of the year for good luck, zest, and well-being for each Sun sign, as well as those times when it would be best to keep your head below the parapet.

1
All You Want to Know About Aries

Your Element—Fire

Fire signs are called the initiators of the zodiac because they don't allow grass to grow under their feet. If a job needs to be done, no one can do it more quickly and effectively than you. However, if the job is a long-winded one that requires persistence, you may have to find someone else to come in and finish it for you. You grasp opportunities when they are offered, and you don't understand those who do not have the courage and initiative to do the same themselves. Your intelligence and courage are to be admired, but you can become arrogant and overbearing with those whom you consider less able than yourself. You are a spendthrift, but you are as likely to spend money on others as on yourself.

Your Quality—Cardinal

There is a kind of self-centeredness about all cardinal sign people, which means it is hard to push you into doing things you don't want to do. You're able to come up with some great ideas, but you may not always be able to carry them out. You take responsibility easily, and you care for those who are weaker than yourself, but if others try to hold you back, you will resist.

Your Ruling Planet—Mars

Mars was once the Roman god of war, so naturally this planet has always been seen as aggressive and dynamic. The ancient Greek version is Ares (or Aries), so this planet and its sign really do fit well together. The actual planet when seen in the sky has a slightly reddish color; it is probably the association between the color red and action and activity that suggested the connection between the planet and the warlike god.

Your Symbol—the Ram

The ram first appeared in ancient Egypt representing the first of the gods, Ammon. This is very apt for the first sign of the zodiac. In ancient times the sign of Aries was also symbolized by the goose, although the origins of that connection have been lost over the centuries.

Your Appearance

There are two kinds of typical Aries looks. One is tall, with well-defined eyebrows and the look of the ram. The other type is small to medium in height and inclined to run to fat with chubby cheeks. You can tend to look more like a sheep than a ram as you get older. Many Aries have a reddish tinge to their hair, rather flat cheekbones, and a small, neat nose. Both types of Aries have a fairly wide face with a good deal of space between the ends of the eyes and brows and the side of the hairline. Many Aries have a mole, scar, or some other mark on the face.

Your Part of the Body

Aries rules the head, eyes, skull, and upper jaw.

Your Good Bits

Your best qualities are energy and initiative, a capacity for hard work, and a love of life.

Your Bad Bits

Your worst qualities are selfishness, impatience, aggression, and a dislike of thoroughness.

Your Love and Sex Style

You prefer to be in a settled relationship, but despite this many of you do spend some years living alone, usually after a divorce. Eventually, you find someone new and hopefully take a more balanced, less-selfish view about partnerships. It is hard for any Arian to do without sex, so if you are in a settled relationship or not, you find ways of experiencing passion and of experimenting with your partner of the moment. Your greatest and deepest love may be for one of your children (rarely for all of them) or possibly for a pet or some other animal.

Your Weaknesses
You love fast vehicles and lots of partners.

Your Food and Drink Weaknesses
You can be a sucker for fast food, alcohol, and creamy dishes.

Your Best Day
In ancient times, Tuesday was ascribed to the Roman god Mars.

Your Worst Day
In theory, Friday is your worst day because it is associated with a planet that is traditionally different from Mars—this being Venus. However, you usually love "thank Goodness it's Friday," because the weekend comes hard on its heels.

Your Colors
The Aries color is bright crimson red.

Your Cities
Birmingham (UK), Boston (USA), Calgary, Denver, Florence, Minneapolis, Naples (Italy), Sydney (Australia).

Your Countries
England, Germany, Indonesia, Japan.

Your Vacations

Anywhere lively where you can sit outside and see the world go by and also spend plenty of time shopping for interesting clothes and things for your home. Some Arians are sun lovers, but others find the heat uncomfortable, especially those of you who have a fair or reddish complexion.

Your Landscapes

You like cities, but also enjoy country areas that can offer plenty of variety.

Your Foods

You are not a particularly fussy eater, but you prefer traditional cooking. You like spicy food when you're in the mood for a change. You must ensure that you don't eat too much junk food or fast food though, because it will affect your health.

Your Herbs

Basil and witch hazel.

Your Tissue Salts

Calcium phosphate, potassium phosphate.

Your Aromatherapy Essence.

Peppermint.

Your Bach Flower Remedy

Vervain.

Your Trees

Thorn and chestnut.

Your Flowers

Honeysuckle.

Your Animals
Vulture, fox, ostrich, leopard, and of course, the sheep or ram.

Your Metal
The metal associated with your sign is iron. Iron has a low melting point, and it was the metal from which weapons were made. Oxidized (rusty) iron is a reddish color.

Your Gems
Aries has various gems associated with it, especially the hard, unyielding diamond and the passionate bloodstone.

Your Mode of Dress
You love anything that is new. Whether your taste is plain or flamboyant, you love new things. You may need to choose designs that disguise a prominent rear end.

Your Careers
You like to work in a large organization, preferably as some kind of team leader. You are attracted to teaching, sports, medicine, and engineering. You are happy to work in a social or life-saving organization such as the police, the armed forces, and the paramilitary, or as a paramedic. Once you have retired, you may take up voluntary work; this is because you like to help others and you can't sit about doing nothing. Oddly enough, many Arians are quite psychic and there are many Arian mediums and clairvoyants.

Your Friends
Honest, energetic, intelligent, and generous people.

Your Enemies
You dislike devious or indecisive types or penny-pinching nitpickers.

Your Attitude to Money
You love the stuff, as long as you have plenty of it to spend just how you want.

Your Favorite Automobile
You love to drive fast and you prefer a fully automatic vehicle that doesn't involve you in much gear changing. Your favorite auto would be a company vehicle that is provided, looked after, and paid for by someone else! If you can't have that, then a secondhand auto would do, especially if it is slightly unusual in some way.

Your Ideal Home
You need plenty of space for all your junk, so a large house that includes a good attic, basement, and a shed at the end of the garden would be nice. You appreciate having a room where you can keep your hobbies and bits and pieces lying around.

Your Preferred Drink
Some Arians are prodigious drinkers; most seem to go in for beer and whisky, although you would probably drink anything that's going. Most Arians are very modest drinkers, preferring a drop of wine with a meal or an occasional spirit drink or cocktail. The odd thing is that many of you have some association with heavy drinking, either because you drink a lot or because others around you are verging on alcoholism.

Your Favorite Meal Out
You love eating out and will eat almost any type of food, especially if it is interesting and well presented.

However, you probably enjoy eating with your friends and family at home even more than going out to restaurants.

Your Night Out
You love to sing, dance, eat, drink, and be merry among friends. You love nothing better than to talk and to have a good laugh.

Your Preferred Activities
You enjoy sport, partying, and making love.

Your Favorite Television Program
None of them. You would rather do anything than sit and watch the television. You are keen on sport though, so that is probably what you watch most.

The Gift You Would Most Appreciate
Arians love gadgets, so a pocket computer game, an electronic desk game, or a new sports car would suit both male and females of the species. Both sexes also love new clothes, so a shopping trip would be very acceptable indeed. Some love to buy sports equipment, tools, camping equipment, interesting jewelry, and unusual ornaments.

The Books You Enjoy
You like to read biography, history, adventure, thrillers, and steamy erotic stories. Male Arians love leafing through newspapers and publications that offer items to buy or to exchange. Female Arians love clothing and household catalogues.

The Music You Enjoy
You love music that has some kind of depth to it and this can be either classical or rock music. You enjoy old songs

and folk music that you can sing along with. Many Arians have excellent singing voices.

The Games and Sports That You Enjoy

You love energetic team games such as cricket, football, baseball, or hockey along with mental games such as chess, cards, or draughts.

Your Potential Health Problems

The eyes: conjunctivitis and squints. The head, including the upper jaw. You can suffer from headaches, sudden infections, accidents, and burns; also reproductive or urinary problems. This sign also rules acts of violence.

Your Lucky Number

One.

Your Money Luck

You can have the occasional windfall but most of your money luck comes as a result of working in a large organization or working for yourself and sticking to the job until your pension comes through.

Your Karmic Lesson

Learn to look after yourself and others; don't rely on others too much, and try to be generous, loving, and sexy.

Success in Love and Compatibility

Aries with Aries

You are both highly sexed, but you both like to take the lead and you both tend to lose your temper if things don't go your way, so a sense of humor will be needed.

Aries with Taurus
Apart from certain exceptional cases, you are too different for real long-term happiness; however, a short-lived relationship might be fun.

Aries with Gemini
This is often a successful combination unless you are selfish and the Gemini is a worrier or a miser.

Aries with Cancer
You are both interested in family life but you may both want to make the major decisions, so arguments are likely. Cancer likes to save money, so this could be a source of friction.

Aries with Leo
You both like to call the shots and you both like to be the boss, so while the sexual highjinks could make this a very exciting affair, the relationship is unlikely to last.

Aries with Virgo
You have so little in common that, unless there are other factors on your horoscopes that make for compatibility, this is hardly worth the bother.

Aries with Libra
This combination often works because Libra likes to follow as long as he or she can respect and believe in you.

Aries with Scorpio
This may make for a very hot and volatile affair, but it is unlikely to work over the long term. At the very least, your fights would keep the neighbors from getting bored.

Aries with Sagittarius

This is likely to be successful, especially where there are shared interests. Your sex life will be extremely interesting as well.

Aries with Capricorn

Capricorn has a stabilizing influence on you and as long as you have shared interests, this could work, but if the Capricorn partner is prone to depression, you will soon fall out.

Aries with Aquarius

This can be successful, because Aquarius ignores your tantrums and gets on with whatever he or she was doing before your explosion.

Aries with Pisces

You may share interests in art, music, or psychic matters, but your tendency to dominate would irritate Pisces, which would lead the more sensitive Pisces to drift away from you.

2

All You Want to Know About
Taurus

Your Element—Earth

You are practical, diligent, hard-working, and are often happiest when doing something useful. You can be relied upon, even though it might take you a while to get around to things. You are thorough and capable, but you cannot stand being harassed or rushed. You have a creative streak and your sensuality means that you know how to make things (and people) look and feel good.

Being shrewd and cautious, you need material and emotional security, and you will put up with a lot in order to get it and keep it. You may appear stingy to outsiders, but this is because you fear poverty. You cling to your family, but being sociable, you don't usually keep outsiders at a distance.

Your Quality—Fixed

Your fixed nature means that it takes you a while before you find the right partner, the right job, or the right place to live, but once you have, you stick to your choices. Sometimes you hang on to things when it would be better to let them go; this can bring you pain in the long run. You are thorough, and you can finish all that you start.

Your Ruling Planet—Venus

Venus is associated with luxury and such activities as eating, drinking, and merrymaking. This is also the planet of love and sensuality.

Your Symbol—the Bull

Myths and legends about this animal go back a long way. It was in the shape of a bull that Jupiter kidnapped Europa and founded the Cretan culture. The Cretans forever afterwards worshiped the bull, calling it the earth-shaker. The bull is a symbol of strength, endurance, and sexuality.

Your Appearance

Taureans come in two shapes, but neither is tall. If you are the lucky slim type, you will never put on weight; if you are the heavy type, you will always have to watch your diet. You usually have lovely hair, eyes, and a clear and glowing skin.

Your Part of the Body

Taurus rules the lower jaw, the throat—including the thyroid gland—the neck, and upper spine.

Your Good Bits

You are thorough in all that you do, careful with money, and very patient. You can put up with a lot, and you don't leave anything half done. You are often brighter than you look! Many Taureans are very sociable and make wonderful hosts and hostesses. Some are fabulous cooks.

Your Bad Bits

You have a reputation for obstinacy and possessiveness. You can be very materialistic and greedy for money, possessions, and food. You can have a rather nasty, sarcastic, and sneering manner that you use to cover feelings of inadequacy, and you can be irritable when you are hungry. You may have a rather silly sense of humor.

Your Love and Sex Style

You are not one for moving from one partner to the next; you are a true family person. Even if you divorce, you will try to look after your ex-partner from a distance. You rarely lose touch with your parents or children either. Sexually, you are sensual and giving, but you don't like partners who demand unusual practices.

Your Weaknesses
Money, food, and possessions.

Your Food and Drink Weaknesses
Cakes and sweets.

Your Best Day
Friday: this is traditionally Venus's day.

Your Worst Day
Tuesday, because this day is ascribed to Mars.

Your Colors
Green and pink.

Your Cities
Dublin, Hastings, Leipzig, Lucerne, Memphis, Ottawa, Parma, St. Louis, Salt Lake City.

Your Countries
Iran, Ireland, Sweden, Switzerland, Turkey.

Your Vacations
Anywhere that is attractive and restful. A Rhine boat trip or a visit to the tulip fields in Holland would be ideal.

Your Landscapes
You enjoy country areas that have plenty of greenery, but many of you also love being on or by the sea.

Your Foods
You love to cook and also to eat, but you are quite particular about what you put into your stomach. You like everything to be fresh and of good quality. You enjoy nice wine too. Apples, peaches, and sweet flavors are traditional favorites for your sign.

Your Herbs
Sorrel.

Your Tissue Salts
Sodium sulfate, sodium phosphate.

Your Aromatherapy Essence
Sandalwood.

Your Bach Flower Remedy
Walnut.

Your Trees
Sycamore and apple.

Your Flowers
Rose, poppy, violet, foxglove, vine, and clover.

Your Animals
Panther, nightingale, small farm animals, and of course, the bull.

Your Metal
Copper. The colors of Taurus are pink and green, and copper is a pinkish metal that oxidizes to green. Copper is made from malachite, a beautiful, deep, rich green stone. Polished copper has always been used for home decoration and for personal ornamentation. Copper bracelets are supposed to keep rheumatism away, so these can be helpful as you get older.

Your Gems
There are various gems associated with your sign. The deep green emerald is an obvious association for your sign, but you may prefer the topaz or the sapphire.

Your Mode of Dress
Conservative, comfortable, and non-flashy.

Your Careers
You love to work with your hands and to build or create things that look good or that has some use, so heavy activities could include farming, gardening, and building. Other careers may include makeup artist, beautician, hairdresser, chef, fashion designer, or photographer. You are interested in finance, so accountancy and banking might appeal. In addition to your artistic interests, you may sing, dance, and act.

Your Friends
You like anyone who has time to sit and chat and who doesn't put you down. You don't care for those who do not appreciate the efforts that you make.

Your Enemies
Know-it-alls who talk a lot and achieve nothing.

Your Attitude to Money
You think that money is made flat so it piles up easier. The more you can invest in your land and property and save for a rainy day the better—until you are seduced by the selection of plants in the garden center, that is.

Your Favorite Automobile
Anything that is large, comfortable, and reliable.

Your Ideal Home
You would prefer a large house with plenty of land around it. The house would ideally be filled with beautiful and collectable items; it should have a large kitchen and a nice dining room for entertaining your many friends.

Your Preferred Drink

Good quality wine or wine-based drinks such as sherry, port or brandy. Taureans are not usually big drinkers, so it is not often that you overdo things and get drunk.

Your Favorite Meal Out

Good-quality food in a good restaurant, preferably a fairly traditional type of meal, such as steak or lamb chops—and a good dessert is a must.

Your Night Out

You enjoy a night at the theater, especially if music is involved, an evening with friends or a formal occasion that requires dressing up. You also enjoy a stroll along the beach or in the countryside and a drink at an interesting country pub.

Your Preferred Activities

You enjoy cooking, gardening, and watching television.

Your Favorite Television Program

You will watch programs about money, or lifestyle programs such as gardening, fixing up your home, dancing, and the arts. Otherwise, you like anything that you can fall asleep in front of!

The Gift You Would Most Appreciate

Taureans of both sexes appreciate beautiful things, so anything attractive that adds a touch of luxury will be most appreciated. You also love music, so tickets to a musical event as well as a couple of CDs go down well. A few bottles of good quality wine or a hamper of exotic food may also be a good gift idea. Ladies appreciate cosmetics, jewelry, comfy furniture, and a nice night out. Both sexes love cellular phones!

The Books You Enjoy

Useful books on gardening, cooking, or homemaking. Also behind-the-scenes stuff, such as autobiographies, history from an insider's view, and investigative matters.

The Music You Enjoy

Melodic classical music, opera, and good pop music, especially anything you can sing along to. Taurus rules the voice, so you could be an excellent singer.

The Games and Sports that You Enjoy

You don't really like games or sports; for exercise, you enjoy dancing and gardening.

Your Potential Health Problems

The lower jaw, lower teeth, and throat (including the thyroid gland). The neck and lower spine are delicate. Some of you gain weight.

Your Lucky Number

Two.

Your Money Luck

You can make money from buying, decorating, and selling property; also from land, farming, building, or as a result of a creative enterprise. Some Taureans gain money by inheriting it.

Your Karmic Lesson

You need to take care of yourself and others and to ensure that you and everyone around you feel comfortable.

Success in Love and Compatibility

Taurus with Aries
This can work, especially if you have interests in common. You would enjoy traveling and homemaking together.

Taurus with Taurus
You either have an instinctive mutual understanding, or you become rivals and fall out after a while.

Taurus with Gemini
Taurus will be a stable and reassuring influence on Gemini, while Gemini will make Taurus laugh and have fun.

Taurus with Cancer
This is a good combination with a similar outlook and attitude to family life, home life, and finances. You may find Cancer a little inclined to cling or to lean on you at times.

Taurus with Leo
Despite the fact that you are both rather obstinate, you can care very deeply for each other. You also both share a fondness for children or animals.

Taurus with Virgo
This should be a success, as you have much in common. What Virgo lacks in domestic skills you supply, and what you lack in attention to detail, Virgo supplies.

Taurus with Libra
Your shared interests and laid-back attitude to life make you compatible. You may share similar careers and a

similar attitude to domestic responsibilities and finances. This is a good combination.

Taurus with Scorpio

This can be very successful due to the fact that you can both commit to a long-term relationship. However, it could be an absolute disaster owing to the fact that both of you are stubborn and inflexible. You may feel that Scorpio wants to hog the limelight.

Taurus with Sagittarius

The only thing you have in common is a fondness for travel, so a true love relationship is unlikely.

Taurus with Capricorn

This is an excellent combination, as you both enjoy homemaking, gardening, and doing things as a family. Neither of you enjoy the company of loud, embarrassing, or messy people, so you can be safe, peaceful, and comfortable.

Taurus with Aquarius

This can be a tense relationship. You have little in common, your thinking processes are different, and you are both stubborn.

Taurus with Pisces

You both appreciate art, music, homemaking, and family life, and you are both sensuous, so this is a good combination.

3

All You Want to Know About Gemini

Your Element—Air

Yours is the element of communication, so you will always choose a job and a lifestyle that keeps you in touch with others and probably also one that takes you from one place to another. You need a variety of interests in your life and plenty of places to go and people to see. You may spend more on the phone than is healthy for your bank balance, but it keeps you sane, so what the heck! Your mind is quick and you can often see solutions to other people's problems, although you are less able to solve your own problems when they arise.

Your Quality—Mutable

You are able to adapt fairly easily to new circumstances and you appreciate a change of scenery from time to time. You don't have a very strong personality, so you are happiest when living and working with people who nurture you and who make you feel good about yourself. You love your family but you need to get away and spend a little time alone on occasion in order to recharge your emotional batteries.

Your Ruling Planet—Mercury

The Roman god Mercury was the swift-witted messenger of the gods. His principal job was to do Jupiter's dirty work and to run errands.

Your Symbol—the Twins

In this case, the heavenly twins, Castor and Pollux. The symbol of the heavenly twins is known in many cultures, including the Native Americans. The Bible emphasizes the rivalry of twins in the story of Cain and Abel.

Your Appearance

While there are some overweight Geminis, most of you are small and slim. You have bright eyes and a ready smile. Your fine hair may be the bane of your life because it can be difficult to control.

Your Part of the Body
Gemini rules the upper respiratory system, the shoulders, arms, wrists, and hands.

Your Good Bits
You have mental agility, adaptability, the ability to communicate, and a witty sense of humor.

Your Bad Bits
You can have a lack of sympathy when others are ill or unhappy. You can all too easily become melancholy and self-absorbed. You may hop from one idea to another. Some Geminis don't know how to tell the truth.

Your Love and Sex Style
You tend to fall in love very deeply, but you can choose selfish or unloving partners. If you can see where you are going wrong after one or two mistakes you will be fine; otherwise you will find yourself expected to act as servant or emotional and physical punching bag to one partner after another. You are surprisingly experimental where sex is concerned, because you can get bored by the same old routine.

Your Weaknesses
You can spend hours chatting on the phone. Geminis who don't smoke make a great fuss about other people's cigarette smoke, because inevitably it drifts across the room toward them.

Your Food and Drink Weaknesses

Some of you go in for alcohol, fast food, and pizza, but others have a total lack of interest in food that leads to anorexia.

Your Best Day

Wednesday, because it is associated with the Roman god Mercury.

Your Worst Day

Friday.

Your Colors

Astrological tradition suggests yellow, black-and-white check, and multicolored mixtures.

Your Cities

Bruges, Kansas City, London, Melbourne, Richmond (USA), San Francisco, Winnipeg.

Your Countries

Indonesia, Japan, Wales.

Your Vacations

You enjoy a good old-fashioned beach holiday where you can soak up the sun. You enjoy any place that has a variety of shops, interesting places to eat out, and also plenty to see.

Your Landscapes

You like cities and interesting old towns in hilly areas.

Your Foods

We are tempted to say a glass of wine, a cup of coffee, a cigarette, and a few vitamin pills, because many Geminis are not really into eating. When you do eat, you prefer something light and tasty. Tradition ascribes beans to your sign but oddly enough, some Geminis hate them.

Your Herbs
Marjoram.

Your Tissue Salts
Calcium sulfate, ferrous phosphate, potassium chloride.

Your Aromatherapy Essence
Eucalyptus.

Your Bach Flower Remedy
Larch.

Your Trees
Nut trees, especially the walnut.

Your Flowers
Tradition suggests that your plants are the lily of the valley, lavender, orchid, and the gladiolus.

Your Animals
Hyena, monkey, parrot, and stork.

Your Metal
Mercury.

Your Gems
There are various gems associated with your sign, including the agate, alexandrite, and onyx.

Your Mode of Dress
Anything that allows you to move around quickly and that is in fashion. High fashion sports clothes are ideal. You love clothes and will spend a lot of money on good

ones, but the real expense comes from your love of accessories.

Your Careers
You can work in any field that involves communication, which may include being a writer, journalist, teacher, telephone operator, or salesperson. Travel is also an important part of many Gemini careers, so you could become a taxi driver, courier, travel agent, cabin crew, or pilot of an airplane.

Your Friends
Your friends must be intelligent, humorous people, who have interesting lives.

Your Enemies
You hate dull, mean, or crabby types, and you have little patience for quiet, introverted people, or spiteful and offensive ones.

Your Attitude to Money
Your symbol of the twins makes you a complex and double-sided personality, and nowhere does this show more than in the way you approach financial matters. You usually ensure that you can pay your bills, but you can go nuts when you are let loose in a shop that sells clothing and accessories.

Your Favorite Automobile
A small, fast sports vehicle suits you best. Even if you have absolutely no money at all, you need to be mobile, and therefore you will put up with any kind of broken-down transport rather than be without wheels.

Your Ideal Home

A home in an area where the air is fresh and there is room for a garden. Plenty of storage space for your vast collection of gadgets and at least three telephones! You also need a maid to do the cleaning and ironing for you, and someone to clean up the mess that your animals leave.

Your Preferred Drink

This is quite an addictive sign and a great many Geminis drink quite heavily. Even light drinkers enjoy spirits, wine, beer, or lager with a meal. Cocktails and mixed drinks are liked too.

Your Favorite Meal Out

Question: what does the Gemini make for dinner? Answer: reservations! You prefer simple foods like fish and chips or salads to overcooked dishes or piles of unidentified mush. Many Geminis enjoy Chinese food because it consists of tasty tidbits. Many of you are vegetarians. Most of you are happy with a drink, a cigarette, and the occasional tomato sandwich to keep you from keeling over.

Your Night Out

You love to dress up in nice clothes, so you like to go to places where you can show them off. You don't like crowds, so a classy restaurant where you can sit with a few friends or a quiet cocktail bar is great. You also enjoy music, so anything from a pop show to a visit to the opera suits you.

Your Preferred Activities

Shopping, talking with friends, spending time with your children and pets.

Your Favorite Television Program

You probably spend more time reading than watching television, but when you do watch, you either choose something intelligent, such as a documentary or an escapist film with a clever plot and a good script.

The Gift You Would Most Appreciate

Stationery of any kind appeals to you, and a good quality pen and pencil set would suit some of you. Airline tickets to a hot place would delight you, as would a hands-on day at a racetrack. You love books, computer equipment, cell phones and electronic address books. Additionally, anything in a clever box or bag, such as makeup, bathroom stuff, or a manicure set, would appeal to you.

The Books You Enjoy

You like to read about people, but you also enjoy reading magazines, newspapers, and psychology and astrology books.

The Music You Enjoy

You like anything with clever or meaningful lyrics and compilations.

The Games and Sports That You Enjoy

Your sports are badminton, tennis, word games, and board games.

Your Potential Health Problems

Your weak points are your hands, arms, shoulders, upper respiratory tract, and the nervous system. Gemini also rules the nervous system and the mind, so any kind of nervous ailment can be expected.

Your Lucky Number
Three.

Your Money Luck

A surprising number of Geminis gain money by marrying a wealthy partner. If this doesn't happen, then you are most likely to work for your wealth.

Your Karmic Lesson

Your job in this lifetime is to be a friend and to communicate with others. You may also need to do something to help those who are worse off than yourself.

Success in Love and Compatibility

Gemini with Aries

This can be a good combination unless Aries is too bossy or selfish. You can think up ideas for Aries to carry out.

Gemini with Taurus

You are so different that it is either a case of opposites attracting, or there is nothing to hold this relationship together.

Gemini with Gemini

You may understand each other completely and create an atmosphere of total harmony, or you can get each other down by both demanding attention at the same time.

Gemini with Cancer

You probably share enough similarities and interests to keep you happy. Cancer will mother you, and this could be just what you most need.

Gemini with Leo

This can work well because you share a great sense of humor, but you can both become extremely downhearted at times, so you must guard against depressing each other.

Gemini with Virgo
You share interests and you may have plenty of patience for each other's worries and neuroses. Virgo's stubborn behavior may aggravate you at times.

Gemini with Libra
This should be an easy relationship as long as you don't expect the world from your Libran partner. You should have a similar sex drive, so that helps things along.

Gemini with Scorpio
This is a poor combination as Scorpio will dominate you and you will use sarcasm in return. It could work for a short-term fling, but that is about all.

Gemini with Sagittarius
Your Sagittarian partner will make you laugh, and you share many interests, so this should be a good one for the long haul. Your partner needs plenty of freedom, so you must avoid clinging too tightly.

Gemini with Capricorn
A similar outlook on family life can make this work, although this is not the easiest of combinations, as Capricorn may seek to dominate you.

Gemini with Aquarius
This is an excellent combination as long as Aquarius is not too detached. You will make your Aquarian partner laugh, and you will certainly have plenty to chat about.

Gemini with Pisces
This can work as you are both adaptable, but Pisces may irritate you, and you may also want more commitment than Pisces can handle.

4

All You Want to Know About Cancer

Your Element—Water

is the element of emotion, and you are certainly sensitive and emotional. Your feelings run deep, and you tend to let your emotions spill over into areas of your life where logic would serve you better. You often make decisions on the spur of the moment based on your feelings at the time, but that you regret later in life.

Your Quality—Cardinal

There is a kind of self-centeredness about all cardinal sign people, which means it is hard to push you into doing things you don't want to do. You're able to come up with some great ideas, but you may not always be able to carry them out. You take responsibility easily, and you care for those who are weaker than yourself, but if others try to hold you back, you will resist.

Your Ruling Planet—the Moon

The Moon represents the feminine principal, and it is connected to the idea of travel and the sea. The Moon is associated with many classical goddesses, including Persephone and Selene, also known as Luna. This sign also relates to Artemis or Diana, the virgin huntress who was the twin sister of Apollo.

Your Symbol—the Crab

The crab has a hard shell and a soft and tasty interior, just like you. It also goes about things in a sideways direction, which you also do on occasion. Legend says that the crab was thrown into the sky for pinching Hercules on the toe while he was involved in one of his difficult labors.

Your Appearance

You are usually of middle height or even a little on the tall side. Some of you gain weight later in life, especially around the top half of your body. Your hair is abundant and healthy, and you have slightly rounded cheeks and a nice smile.

Your Part of the Body

The lungs, breast, and rib cage; also the stomach and digestive organs.

Your Good Bits

You are a good listener and a kindhearted and sympathetic friend. Your family relies on you and friends can always count on you.

Your Bad Bits

You can be moody and bad tempered without being able to explain why. You can cling to your family.

Your Love and Sex Style

You love every member of your family, even if they get on your nerves! You can even take on step- or grandchildren and bring them up as your own. In love, you are passionate and caring but you can also be surprisingly demanding. Some of you show your love by cooking for your partner; others enjoy pleasing a partner in bed. You are not notably adventurous in bed. Love and affection count for more with you than sexual fireworks.

Your Weaknesses

You worry about everything—especially money—and you can be a miser at times.

Your Food and Drink Weaknesses

You can overindulge on chocolate, sweet desserts, bread, and things to spread on it. You may not bother with alcohol, but you may like the occasional glass of medium-sweet wine.

Your Best Day

Monday, which is traditionally the moon's day.

Your Worst Day

Wednesday.

Your Colors

White, silver, and all pearly or oyster shades.

Your Cities

Atlanta, Amsterdam, Christchurch, Manchester, New York, Vancouver, Venice.

Your Countries

Holland, Mauritius, New Zealand, Scotland.
Although some astrologers suggest Gemini or even Sagittarius for the USA, we think it is Cancerian, because it was born on the fourth of July.

Your Vacations

You love being close to or on water, especially the sea. You are wary of strange foods, so you tend to visit traditional places that don't spring dietary surprises on you.

Your Landscapes

Green areas near water and places that offer sea views.

Your Foods

Cancerians love to eat, and you prefer a properly cooked meal. Your stomach is delicate, so you may prefer not to eat highly spiced dishes. Chocolate and other sweet things appeal to you, as does a traditional Christmas dinner. You are not much of a drinker, but you appreciate a little fine wine on occasion.

Your Herbs

Rosemary and comfrey.

Your Tissue Salts

Calcium fluoride, silica, sodium phosphate.

Your Aromatherapy Essence

Coriander.

Your Bach Flower Remedy

Honeysuckle.

Your Trees

Traditionally willow, but also the mangrove, because this tree grows near or in water; the Australian paper-bark tree as well, for much the same reason.

Your Flowers

Acanthus, lotus (water lily), and wild flowers. Cancerians have a good memory, therefore, rosemary for remembrance.

Your Animals

Crab, lobster, tortoise, owl, otter, cuckoo, and frog.

Your Metal

Silver.

Your Gems
The pearl and also mother of pearl.

Your Mode of Dress
You favor rather formal clothes in attractive colors such as lavender or pale greens and blues. Once you are out of your teens and early twenties, you avoid funky or strange garments.

Your Careers
You like small-scale business, so owning your own shop may appeal. Also antique dealer, teacher, nurse, chef, hotelier, manager, and anything related to teaching and caring for small children or older people.

Your Friends
You like gentle, home-loving types and also business people who speak your language. You prefer people who understand your need for privacy.

Your Enemies
You dislike rude, brash, noisy, intrusive, and unhelpful people.

Your Attitude to Money
Most of the time you are careful to the point of stinginess, but you can spend heavily on travel and also on your loved ones.

Your Favorite Automobile
This would probably be a minibus that holds the family, the dogs, and all the shopping. You cannot cope with a small vehicle, as it would never be able to carry all your junk.

Your Ideal Home

You like living with family members in a happy atmosphere. Otherwise, you want to live close to your family or near another family that you can become attached to. You prefer an older building, and when you find the right one you tend to stay put. You may add on a mother-in-law apartment for visiting relatives and friends.

Your Preferred Drink

You are not much of a drinker, so you are probably happiest with a cup of tea.

Your Favorite Meal Out

You are an excellent cook and thus also a discriminating diner. You probably enjoy French food, made with the freshest ingredients and cooked to perfection. You would not hesitate to ask for the recipe.

Your Night Out

You enjoy going to the theater, so any kind of show, play, musical, opera, or performance goes down well·with you. Otherwise you enjoy a trip to the cinema.

Your Preferred Activities

Relaxing with friends and your loved ones, and also cooking for them. You love being with people who make you laugh. You also love to travel with people who make you happy.

Your Favorite Television Program

You enjoy soap operas, history, nature, geography, wildlife, and travel documentaries. You also like programs about the strange things that people do.

The Gift You Would Most Appreciate

Cancerians are supposed to be home loving, and so you are. Nevertheless, you love to get away, so tickets to an outing, a trip, or any kind of event suits you nicely. You love music, so tickets to a show or a pop concert would also be nice. Gadgets for the kitchen and nice tableware are also appreciated. You also love albums, silver ornaments, and jewelry. Also antiques, coins, or anything else that can be collected.

The Books You Enjoy

You like stories that are set in exotic locations. You also enjoy reading history, historical romance, murder mysteries, and books on travel or the armed services.

The Music You Enjoy

You love nostalgic music that brings back pleasant memories, along with soft pop or popular classical music.

The Games and Sports That You Enjoy

You like football, walking, and exploring. You have an excellent memory so games of strategy such as Othello, Connect Four, and card games such as bridge or poker may appeal.

Your Potential Health Problems

Your weak spots are the chest, thorax, lower lungs, and breasts and also the stomach and upper digestive system. Poor eating habits may cause trouble. You may retain body fluids.

Your Lucky Number

Four.

Your Money Luck

You can inherit money or be given it by other members of your family. Otherwise you gain money by buying and selling property.

Your Karmic Lesson

Your karmic destiny is to take care of others and to make a nice home, as well as to stretch your imagination by reading, thinking, talking, and traveling to interesting places. You should try to control your moods and to avoid making decisions that are based on the way that you feel at any moment in time.

Success in Love and Compatibility

Cancer with Aries

You share a love of home life and concern for the family, so this can be good match. Aries will try to dominate you, but you won't allow your partner to get away with too much of that kind of behavior.

Cancer with Taurus

You have lots in common and a similar attitude to love, sex, family life, and money, so this looks very good indeed. You will have some wonderful vacations together.

Cancer with Gemini

You mother Gemini, and Gemini likes being mothered. In return, Gemini will make you laugh, give you plenty of attention, and get you out of the house from time to time.

Cancer with Cancer
This combination is either extremely harmonious, or else you are too alike to keep each other interested for very long.

Cancer with Leo
This should not work at all, but oddly enough it does. You both love family life and you both need the stability that the other can offer.

Cancer with Virgo
You are both caring and somewhat self-sacrificial, so you should get along quite easily. However, Virgo is quiet and logical, so your partner may find your emotionalism hard to cope with.

Cancer with Libra
You like to be in charge and to make decisions, and Libra is indecisive, so this could work well. You will either be content together or argue fiercely.

Cancer with Scorpio
You are both intuitive and apt to make decisions based on the way you feel at any moment in time. As long as your emotions run in tandem, this can work as long as Scorpio is not too domineering.

Cancer with Sagittarius
You have so little in common that this stands very little chance of working. You like to cling while Sagittarius needs freedom, and your priorities are utterly different.

Cancer with Capricorn
This can be an excellent combination, as you have much in common. You may find it easiest if you are the homemaker and Capricorn the money-earner.

Cancer with Aquarius
You will find it extremely difficult to understand each other, and your thought processes are different, so this is not an easy mixture.

Cancer with Pisces
You are both intuitive and sensitive, and you think in similar ways, so this might work. However, Pisces needs more freedom than you might wish to give.

5

All You Want to Know About Leo

Your Element—Fire

Fire signs are called the initiators of the zodiac because they don't allow grass to grow under their feet. If a job needs to be done, no one can do it more quickly and effectively than you. However, if the job is a long-winded one that requires persistence, you may have to find someone else to come in and finish it for you. You grasp opportunities when they are offered, and you don't understand those who do not have the courage and initiative to do the same themselves. Your intelligence and courage are to be admired, but you can become arrogant and overbearing with those whom you consider less able than yourself. You are a spendthrift, but you are as likely to spend money on others as on yourself.

Your Quality—Fixed

Your fixed nature means that it takes you a while before you find the right partner, the right job, or the right place to live, but once you have, you stick to your choices. Sometimes you hang on to things when it would be better to let them go; this can bring you pain in the long run. You are thorough, and you can finish all that you start.

Your Ruling Planet—the Sun

The Sun is associated with the Roman god Apollo, who was the god of music, poetry, prophecy, reason, light, and healing.

Your Symbol—the Lion

This commemorates the first of the labors of Hercules, which was the defeat of the Nemean lion. The lion has always been associated with strong men—Samson also fought a lion. Many Leos actually look a bit like the king of the jungle.

Your Appearance

Typical Leos are medium or slightly less in height and usually medium in weight as well, although they may put on weight later in life. Their best feature is likely to be their hair, which is abundant and slightly wavy. Both sexes like long hair when young, but females may cut their hair shorter later for the sake of convenience while men tend to get a little thin on top. Leo eyes are small and sometimes quite deep set and somewhat simian in style, so female Leos usually wear a lot of eye makeup to make their eyes look larger.

Your Part of the Body

The parts of the body associated with Leo are the spine, heart, arteries, and circulation.

Your Good Bits

You are honest, decent, hard-working, and a good organizer. You rarely give up or give in to despair. You are extremely generous and affectionate, and you don't tell others what they should do or how they should live.

Your Bad Bits

You can be arrogant and bad tempered when you don't get your own way or when you are fatigued or hungry. You are also self-centered and sometimes extravagant.

Your Love and Sex Style

You are one of the most affectionate signs of the zodiac, so you can give a great deal of love to those whom you care about. You are also a good friend and a wonderful parent. You also need a lot of affection and you demand loyalty and a high standard of behavior from a partner—perhaps too high in some cases. You are extremely highly sexed, but you get tired quickly, so you may not be inclined to make love if you are working too hard in other areas of your life.

Your Weaknesses
You enjoy being the center of attention and also being the boss.

Your Food and Drink Weaknesses
You are a sucker for smoked salmon, Chinese food, chocolate eclairs, sushi, and anything that is expensive. You are not really into alcohol, but you may enjoy the occasional glass of wine, sweet liqueur, or cocktail.

Your Best Day
Sunday: this is the sun's day.

Your Worst Day
Saturday.

Your Colors
Gold, yellow, creamy shades, and orange.

Your Cities
Blackpool, Bombay, Chicago, Damascus, Labrador City (Canada), Los Angeles, Portsmouth (UK), Prague, Philadelphia, Rome.

Your Countries
Czech Republic, France, Italy, Romania, Slovakia.

Your Vacations
Anywhere that is expensive, sophisticated, and luxurious. The Raffles Hotel in Singapore or a trip on the QE2 would do nicely.

Your Landscapes
Wide open spaces, mountains, forests, and green valleys.

Your Foods
Astrological tradition suggests saffron and citrus fruits because of their golden or yellow color. You are not a particularly fussy eater, as you can enjoy anything that is beautifully cooked.

Your Herbs
Chamomile, saffron, rosemary.

Your Tissue Salts
Magnesium phosphate, calcium phosphate.

Your Aromatherapy Essence
Garlic.

Your Bach Flower Remedy
Vine.

Your Trees
Ash and palm.

Your Flowers
Marigold, nasturtium, sunflower, and cyclamen.

Your Animals
Lion, starfish, crocodile, swan, peacock.

Your Metal
Gold.

Your Gems
There are various gems associated with your sign, such as the diamond, zircon, ruby, sardonyx, and tiger's eye.

Your Mode of Dress

You love to wear classy, colorful clothes—preferably with designer labels.

Your Careers

You are not comfortable when working under others or as part of a team, so you must be in charge. Yours is the sign of the entrepreneur or manager, but you can also shine in any creative or artistic field, especially if it includes performing or teaching. You can work with children or in any field that is glamorous and that carries a sense of status.

Your Friends

You prefer to keep company with interesting and even somewhat outrageous people who achieve success in their own field.

Your Enemies

You can't stand bullies, whiners, or dull and pompous people, or those who try to upstage you.

Your Attitude to Money

You certainly know how to spend lots of money in great style, so you ensure that you also earn lots of money in great style. The biggest drain on your resources comes from your amazing generosity to your friends and loved ones.

Your Favorite Automobile

The most expensive and best-appointed vehicle will do nicely. Better still, a sober vehicle for work and a fun one for weekends.

Your Ideal Home

A large, luxurious home in a nice area would suit you. Your home is neither untidy nor surgically clean—it is comfortable with excellent quality goods and furnishings that you live with for as long as possible before replacing. However, your electrical and hi-fi equipment is usually brand new. There must be a garden or play area for your children and their friends.

Your Preferred Drink

Most Leos can't drink much alcohol, and many are teetotalers. If you do drink, it is likely to be nice wine or perhaps a "short" with a mixer and plenty of ice. A glass of champagne on special occasions usually goes down well too, but your favorite drink is probably tea or coffee.

Your Favorite Meal Out

You enjoy the best of the best, and that includes good service, excellent presentation, and clean linen. Many Leos enjoy a buffet or a salad bar.

Your Night Out

You love to have a good laugh with your friends, and the setting is less important than the company as far as you are concerned. Otherwise, you enjoy the theater or a walk in an attractive park on a summer's night.

Your Preferred Activities

You enjoy playing light sports, traveling, and being with your family. You also enjoy gardening and homemaking.

Your Favorite Television Program

You are too busy living to bother much with the television, but when you do watch it must be something interesting. You have no patience for soap operas or "reality" shows where stupid people are locked up with others for a week until they start screaming at each other.

The Gift You Would Most Appreciate
Leos love luxury, and gold is their lucky metal, so gold jewelry or a gold watch would please you. You might appreciate a year's membership to an up-market health or country club. Another great gift is a holiday in the sun.

The Books You Enjoy
You love a good read, so novels that have a large scope appeal to you. You enjoy adventure stories, science fiction, thrillers, murder mysteries, and the occasional romantic story.

The Music You Enjoy
Lively music, light classical music, dance tunes, romantic pop music.

The Games and Sports That You Enjoy
Leos are often keen on swimming, but you also enjoy tennis and badminton. You love to dance, and you may take lessons so that you can do this well.

Your Potential Health Problems
Your potentially troublesome areas are the spine, the heart, the arteries, and circulation.

Your Lucky Number
Five.

Your Money Luck
You work for your money. Small windfalls can come your way, but in general you gain wealth by your own efforts.

Your Karmic Lesson

You need to get over any childhood hangups and shyness and push yourself into the limelight. You need to give love and to find it, but most of all you need to learn to love yourself. You also need children or pets that you can love to distraction.

Success in Love and Compatibility

Leo with Aries

You are both extremely competitive, and you will each struggle to be top dog, so this is not a comfortable long-term situation—but a short-term love affair would be exciting.

Leo with Taurus

This might work in some cases, but Taurus is slow and apt to be content with life without making the effort to do more or to become more, and this could irritate you.

Leo with Gemini

This can be a nice combination as long as neither is too restless and as long as you don't both become downhearted at the same time.

Leo with Cancer

Technically speaking this should not work at all, as Cancer is too emotional for you, but your shared interests in family life can compensate for any occasional problems that you may experience.

Leo with Leo

Frankly, this works better as a friendship than as a long-term love relationship, probably because you are too similar and both want to be the boss.

Leo with Virgo

As long as Virgo is not neurotic and self-obsessed, this can work, and at least you will make each other laugh.

Leo with Libra

There is a tremendous sexual attraction here, but Libra's habit of switching off and withdrawing into a kind of dream world might put you off. There could also be a fight for supremacy.

Leo with Scorpio

Oddly enough, this match is often very successful, as you both like to make a commitment to family life, but Scorpio can go on about things sometimes, and this bores you.

Leo with Sagittarius

This can work as long as the Sagittarian has some common sense and is prepared to commit to the long haul—otherwise it would make a fun short-term fling.

Leo with Capricorn

As long as the Capricorn is sociable and outgoing, this works fine, but if your partner is the workaholic depressive type, you will soon get bored.

Leo with Aquarius

You are both stubborn, but if your thinking is along similar lines you can make a success of this one. Aquarius is less interested in children and family life than you are.

Leo with Pisces

Both of you are creative and attracted to show biz and glamour, so you may have many shared interests, but Pisces' habit of drinking or escapism will irritate you.

6

All You Want to Know About Virgo

Your Element—Earth

You are practical, diligent, hardworking, and are often happiest when doing something useful. You can be relied upon even though it might take you a while to get around to things. You are thorough and capable, but you cannot stand being harassed or rushed. You have a creative streak and your sensuality means that you know how to make things (and people) look and feel good.

Being shrewd and cautious, you need material and emotional security, and you will put up with a lot in order to get it and keep it. You may appear stingy to outsiders, but this is because you fear poverty. You cling to your family, but being sociable, you don't usually keep outsiders at a distance.

Your Quality—Mutable

You are able to adapt fairly easily to new circumstances, and you appreciate a change of scenery from time to time. You don't have a very strong personality, so you are happiest when living and working with people who nurture you and make you feel good about yourself. You love your family, but you occasionally need to get away and spend a little time alone in order to recharge your emotional batteries.

Your Ruling Planet—Mercury

Mercury was the messenger of the gods who also did Jupiter's dirty work for him. He was the god of travelers, healing, of magic, and also of thieves.

Your Symbol—the Virgin

This represents the mother goddess who presided over the harvesting of food. To think of Virgo as a prudish old maid is a mistake, because she is only one of the aspects of the great goddess or mother figures of mythology. Perhaps this is a girl who will be a mother at some future date, but who might also be a particularly loving big sister. This sign is also associated with the harvest and with the storage of foodstuffs.

Your Appearance

You may be slightly above average height and your habit of holding your head up gives you a stately manner. Your bone structure is good, so as long as you don't put on too much weight later in life, you can continue to look good well into old age.

Your Part of the Body

Your sign rules the lower digestive system and the bowels. It also concerns the skin, nervous system, and the mind.

Your Good Bits

You are kindhearted and hardworking, and you have the patience needed to cope with detailed craftwork. You are a great conversationalist and you have a wonderful sense of humor.

Your Bad Bits

You can be fussy, critical, and a hypochondriac, and you are prone to tell others how they should live.

Your Love and Sex Style

You show your love for others by doing things for them in preference to showing outright affection. You are the most loyal and courageous friend in the zodiac. Sexually, you can be quite experimental and more promiscuous than most people would imagine.

Your Weaknesses

You are prone to self-punishment, low self-esteem, and being far too quick to criticize yourself and others. You can be sarcastic and hurtful if you feel hurt yourself.

Your Food and Drink Weaknesses

You can indulge in cookies and small cakes—also chocolate when you feel depressed. If you are at all into alcohol, you seem to go for lager or pilsner types of beer or vodka.

Your Best Day

Wednesday: this is associated with the Roman god Mercury.

Your Worst Day

Thursday.

Your Colors

Navy blue, muted greens, mulberry, browns, gray, and pastel shades.

Your Cities

Cheltenham, Heidelberg, Jerusalem, Paris, Phoenix, Reading, Saskatoon (Canada).

Your Countries

Canada, Greece, West Indies.

Your Vacations

You need to go to a relaxing place where you can switch off from work and worries. However, you are easily bored, so you like to visit interesting places.

Your Landscapes

You love gardens, pretty villages, and places that have some history attached to them.

Your Foods

Some Virgos are extremely fussy about food and many are vegetarians. Others are not at all fussy, enjoying everything except for one or two things that you were forced to eat in childhood.

Your Herbs

Parsley and dill.

Your Tissue Salts

Potassium sulfate, silica, sodium chloride.

Your Aromatherapy Essence

Orange.

Your Bach Flower Remedy

Rock water.

Your Trees

Nut trees, especially hazel.

Your Flowers

Cornflowers, small brightly colored flowers, snowdrop, lily, and narcissus.

Your Animals

Squirrel, greyhound, weasel, swallow.

Your Metal

Mercury.

Your Gems

There are various gems associated with your sign, including the sardonyx, diamond, and the chrysolite.

Your Mode of Dress

You dress in a neat and smart style, preferring casual or sporty clothes that don't get in your way or hold you up. Many Virgos suffer from painful feet, so good shoes are a must.

Your Careers

You love to serve others. You also have an interest in health and healing, so many of you work in the medical field or even in that of spiritual healing. Other careers might be those of nutritionist, writer, teacher, healer, secretary, skilled manual work, art, computer programmer, and astrologer.

Your Friends

You appreciate logical and intelligent people who have a good sense of humor and who work hard for what they get in life.

Your Enemies

You dislike materialistic or unrealistic people and also those who are rude, overcritical, abrupt, or who seek to put you down.

Your Attitude to Money

Sometimes you have money and at other times you don't, but you always manage to get by somehow, perhaps by taking on extra work of some kind.

Your Favorite Automobile

Your sign is ruled by Mercury, the fleet-footed messenger of the gods, and Virgo is bracketed by (and infected by) expansive Leo and irresponsible Libra. Therefore you probably tend to choose something fast, efficient, and way out of your price range.

Your Ideal Home
You like houses with enough room for a separate library or office. You enjoy having a garden as long as it isn't too large for you to keep up, because you would hate to see it go to seed. You might choose to live in a flat as long as there was a nice view from the window.

Your Preferred Drink
Many Virgos are beer enthusiasts and some search out special beers that are brewed by small local breweries. Otherwise you are either not fussy as long as there is something around to drink, or you don't drink any alcohol at all.

Your Favorite Meal Out
You may be a very fussy eater, limiting yourself to a small choice of foods. Otherwise, you will eat anything that is familiar to you.

Your Night Out
You like the theater and the opera, but you also enjoy a quiz evening in a pub. Some enjoy playing cards or chess with a group of like-minded people.

Your Preferred Activities
Yours is not a particularly active sign in the sporting sense, so you prefer quiet pursuits such as reading, listening to music, or gossiping with your many friends. Many of you enjoy cooking for your friends, because you enjoy the creative aspect of this.

Your Favorite Television Program

You enjoy strange and clever programs that get you thinking. You may also enjoy children's television, quizzes, game shows, and comedies. Your sense of humor means that you love comedy programs.

The Gift You Would Most Appreciate

You have many interests, and anything that reflects these would suit you. Items such as sports equipment, books on your special subject, or gardening tools might do the trick. Many Virgos enjoy cooking, so kitchen equipment or recipe books are acceptable. You like nice clothes and bathroom items, desk organizers, and videos.

The Books You Enjoy

History, factual books, and "did-you-know" type reference books, philosophy, and intellectual books. You also like stories of pure imagination, such as science fiction.

The Music You Enjoy

You appreciate jazz and classical music; cool, clever music of any kind.

The Games and Sports That You Enjoy

Chess, quizzes, scrabble, board games, and crosswords. You like walking and exploring alone or with a friend. Sports as such don't interest you much, although you may possibly like games of skill such as snooker or golf.

Your Potential Health Problems

Your weak areas are the lower digestive system, intestines and bowels. Others are the skin, nervous system, and the mind. Fad diets could possibly affect your health badly.

Your Lucky Number
Six.

Your Money Luck
You work for your money, but you can receive small windfalls from time to time. Some of you can profit by marrying money.

Your Karmic Lesson
You are bound to spend some part of your life sacrificing your own needs for those of others.

Success in Love and Compatibility

Virgo with Aries
Aries' impulsiveness and hot temper will upset you, and you would soon feel squashed and dominated, so this is not an affair that we would recommend.

Virgo with Taurus
You have much in common, although you will run rings around Taurus intellectually while your partner will be more creative than you are. As long as Taurus is happy with that situation, all will be well.

Virgo with Gemini
You could be happy together as long as neither of you is too much of a worrier. You are very similar in many ways, and you can both adapt well to new situations.

Virgo with Cancer
You are both caring types and you share many interests, so this is a good match. Cancer will encourage you to talk over your problems while you will stimulate your partner's intellect.

Virgo with Leo

This works well because practicality allied to Leo's creativity can make quite a good match. You both enjoy home life and entertaining, so your home could be full of laughter.

Virgo with Virgo

As with all same-sign relationships, this is either great or competitive, particularly as you are both rather stubborn.

Virgo with Libra

You will have a have a hard time pinning the Libran down and you may find yourself arguing about relatively unimportant matters, so this is not a comfortable match.

Virgo with Scorpio

You both have unresolved issues left over from your childhoods, and this will either give you things in common or put you at odds with each other. Scorpio might try to dominate you and you will dig in your heels.

Virgo with Sagittarius

You share a great sense of humor, and you both need space in your lives, so this can work quite well. However, Sagittarius may be less interested in a long-term relationship than you are.

Virgo with Capricorn

You have a certain amount in common and you are both practical, but you are less interested in looking after your parents and in-laws than Capricorn is. In addition, Capricorn may depress you or try to dominate you.

Virgo with Aquarius

This is not an easy relationship, as you both have your own ways of going about things. Aquarius's vagueness may irritate you, while your partner may find your chatter annoying.

Virgo with Pisces

You tend to take on people who need to be rescued. Pisces definitely needs this, but once you have solved one of Pisces' problems, your partner will present you with another. You could become frustrated with this in the long run.

7

All You Want to Know About Libra

Your Element—Air

Yours is the element of communication, so you will always choose a job and a lifestyle that keeps you in touch with others and that takes you from place to place. You need a variety of interests in your life, with plenty of places to go and people to see. You may spend more time on the phone than is healthy for your bank balance, but talking to others keeps you sane, so what the heck! Your mind is quick, and you can often see solutions to other people's problems, although you are less able to solve your own problems when they arise.

Your Quality—Cardinal

There is a kind of self-centeredness about all cardinal sign people, which means it is hard to push you into doing things you don't want to do. You're able to come up with some great ideas, but you may not always be able to carry them out. You take responsibility easily, and you care for those who are weaker than yourself, but if others try to hold you back, you will resist.

Your Ruling Planet—Venus

Venus was the Roman goddess of love and romance. Venus is also associated with luxury and such activities as eating, drinking, lovemaking, and merrymaking.

Your Symbol—the scales

When writing in the first century A.D. the poet Manilius said of this sign, "Day and night are weighed in Libra's scales, equal a while, at last the night prevails." This suggests the order of light and darkness. The scales obviously have something to do with weighing and measuring and also the legal profession. Librans like to weigh up all sides of an argument before making a decision.

Your Appearance

You are one of the luckier signs of the zodiac where looks are concerned, because Librans run from being merely attractive to very good looking indeed. Your pleasant smile and manner also helps you to look good. Caucasian Librans' complexions tend to run from fair to medium in coloring with pale skin. In all other races your good looks and your large, expressive eyes mark you out as a beauty.

Your Part of the Body

Your traditional body parts are the soft organs of the bladder and kidneys. Libra also rules the ability to move and walk, and it can be associated with the lower spine.

Your Good Bits

You are pleasant, charming, and friendly but also fair minded and a good arbitrator.

Your Bad Bits

You can be lazy, indecisive, and totally unrealistic. You can argue the hind leg off a donkey when you feel like doing so.

Your Love and Sex Style

You can be one of the sexiest members of the zodiac and you are incredibly experimental when you are in the mood. However, you are fussy about your sexual partners and you would prefer to go without sex than to jump into bed with just anybody. If you find the right partner you will stay with him or her, although you may not always be faithful. Many of you try marriage a couple of times and then end up living happily alone.

Your Weaknesses

You enjoy sex, pleasure, and luxury.

Your Food and Drink Weaknesses

You can be too fond of alcohol, rich, expensive foods, and scrumptious desserts. If you start to drink, it can end in a real binge if you are not careful.

Your Best Day

Friday: this is traditionally Venus's day.

Your Worst Day

Wednesday.

Your Colors

Sky blue, leaf green, and pink.

Your Cities

Antwerp, Copenhagen, Frankfurt, Indianapolis, Lisbon, Montreal, Nottingham, Sacramento, Vienna.

Your Countries

Austria, Argentina, Burma, Japan, Tibet.

Your Vacations

You enjoy spending your vacation in luxurious surroundings where you can be sure of good food and excellent service. If there is a chance to flirt with the locals, so much the better! You also enjoy short city breaks.

Your Landscapes

Open countryside, the seaside, along with sunny, fresh, and breezy places. You also like cities with all their sophisticated attractions.

Your Foods

You love to eat out in good restaurants. At home you prefer small, nicely presented dishes to great heaps of food simply slapped onto the plate. Astrological tradition suggests that the cherry and the pomegranate resonate with your sign.

Your Herbs
Mint and aloe.

Your Tissue Salts
Sodium phosphate, potassium phosphate.

Your Aromatherapy Essence
Bergamot.

Your Bach Flower Remedy
Olive.

Your Trees
Cypress.

Your Flowers
Roses.

Your Animals
Rabbit, small deer, and the pelican.

Your Metal
Copper. The colors for Venus are pink and green, and copper is an attractive, pink-colored metal that turns green when it oxidizes. Copper is made from malachite, a deep green stone.

Your Gems
There a number of gems associated with your sign, including the sapphire, emerald, and jade.

Your Mode of Dress

You love looking good and prefer to buy expensive, tasteful, elegant clothes than to wear funky or flashy ones.

Your Careers

You may work as a lawyer, arbitrator, counselor, designer, decorator, personnel officer, or restaurateur.

Your Friends

You appreciate logical and intelligent people who are also attractive, amusing, and successful. You enjoy the company of independent people and those who can take care of you.

Your Enemies

You cannot stand scruffy, loud, and coarse types.

Your Attitude to Money

You can do without if you have to, but you usually ensure that you don't have to. Your innate sense of style means that you are inexorably drawn to the nicest and most expensive item in the shop.

Your Favorite Automobile

Given half a chance, you definitely go for something that you cannot afford, like a large and fast Jaguar. You are more concerned with the appearance of the vehicle and its state of internal cleanliness than the type of engine that it has.

Your Ideal Home

Large rooms without too much clutter. Elegant refined decor with clever and decorative ornaments. You must have music playing in most of the rooms. If you can put on an extension for the children and your other relatives that would be great; otherwise you are careful whom you invite to stay.

Your Preferred Drink
You enjoy sophisticated drinks such as cocktails, good wines, and Southern Comfort. Some Librans are fond of seeking out traditional ales and beers.

Your Favorite Meal Out
You enjoy dining out in posh, expensive, impressive surroundings with music playing in the background. Many Librans enjoy interesting, novel, and very spicy foods.

Your Night Out
You enjoy a meal out with friends where you can enjoy some good gossip.

Your Preferred Activities
You enjoy making love, watching television, eating out, and taking vacations in nice places.

Your Favorite Television Program
You prefer to be out and about than watching television but if you do watch, you may prefer a biography, a dramatized documentary, a romantic film, or something about your own special interests.

The Gift You Would Most Appreciate
You love beauty and luxury, so good clothes, something attractive for the home, or nice cosmetics would please you. Ladies would appreciate a day out at a health and beauty center, followed by a visit to a hairdresser. Males enjoy good-looking status symbols, such as a good briefcase, desk set, or a smart watch. Artistic ornaments

and craft items appeal to you, and you love to be given something expensive and stylish to wear.

The Books You Enjoy

You may prefer watching television to reading. However, you do like magazines and newspapers because you like to keep up with whatever is going on in the world. Picture books appeal and anything romantic or that is about your special interest.

The Music You Enjoy

You love clever pop music and melodic music. You may also like certain types of jazz and light classical music.

The Games and Sports That You Enjoy

You might play golf, tennis, bowling, aerobics, dancing, and flying light aircraft.

Your Potential Health Problems

Your weak areas are the soft organs such as the pancreas, bladder, and kidneys. You can also experience problems with movement due to problems with the lower spine or the neck area.

Your Lucky Number
Seven.

Your Money Luck

Despite the fact that you are not a notably hard worker, you can be extremely successful in your career, and this brings money your way. Otherwise your family will help you out when you need money, and you can also marry someone who earns or has money.

Your Karmic Lesson

To take people as they are and to mediate between those who are in dispute. Your role is to be a peacemaker and to have an easy, comfortable life if at all possible.

Success in Love and Compatibility

Libra with Aries

This is a common combination that succeeds over the long term. Libra's laid-back attitude works well with Aries' energy, and you don't usually compete in the same areas of life.

Libra with Taurus

You have so much in common that this is a very comfortable arrangement. You both like to feed and entertain others, so your home will be a happy and sociable place.

Libra with Gemini

You are able to put Gemini's mind at ease, so this can be a pleasant and easygoing combination. You both love to socialize so you can expect life to be full of fun.

Libra with Cancer

Cancer may be too clinging for your taste and also too prone to bring other family members into every corner of your life.

Libra with Leo

This can be an extremely passionate partnership, but you love to argue and Leo takes things to heart, while you think a row is nothing more than verbal aerobics.

Libra with Virgo

Your flirtatious nature may put Virgo on edge and Virgo's fussiness may get you down. This would take a good deal of work.

Libra with Libra

Oddly enough, Librans can be quite different from each other, so there can be enough to keep you interested. If you are too alike, then you would be better as friends than lovers.

Libra with Scorpio

Scorpio is too possessive for your tastes and your tendency to flirt will put Scorpio on edge in a big way. You could enjoy a passionate short-term affair.

Libra with Sagittarius

There may be an initial attraction, but this wears off fairly quickly because you are both apt to drift away and to become involved with other people.

Libra with Capricorn

This is a good business partnership, but Capricorn will get on your nerves on a personal level after a while.

Libra with Aquarius

This can be a very successful relationship, as neither of you seeks to possess the other. You both love to talk things over and to discuss politics or ideas, so there would be friendship along with a strong sexual link.

Libra with Pisces

This might make a fun affair, but neither of you are likely to stay around for long, as other attractions could prove irresistible.

8

All You Want to Know About Scorpio

Your Element—Water

This is the element of emotion, and you are certainly sensitive and emotional. Your feelings run deep, and you tend to let your emotions spill over into areas of your life where logic would serve you better. You often make decisions on the spur of the moment based on your feelings at the time, but that you regret later in life.

Your Quality—Fixed

Your fixed nature means that it takes you a while before you find the right partner, the right job, or the right place to live, but once you have, you stick to your choices. Sometimes you hang on to things when it would be better to let them go; this can bring you pain in the long run. You are thorough, and you can finish all that you start.

Your Ruling Planet—Pluto

Pluto, the Roman god of the underworld, is associated with great wealth, most of which is hidden underground. Pluto also rules union with others, birth, death, and sex. Before Pluto was discovered, Scorpio was assigned to Mars, the red planet associated with the Roman god of war.

Your Symbol—the Scorpion

The scorpion once made the mistake of stinging the giant Orion, who threw him into the sky where he now occupies an area as far as he could possibly be from the constellation of Orion. The scorpion turns its sting onto itself if it feels threatened. The ancient symbol for your sign was once the eagle. This denotes the higher side of Scorpio, which can soar above everything that is base, coarse, and petty.

Your Appearance

There are various types of Scorpio appearance that range from small to medium height, a slim figure and a strong bone structure. Others can run to fat and have a wide face with very widely spaced eyes.

Your Part of the Body

The sexual organs, the lower stomach, lower spine, the groin, blood, and eyes.

Your Good Bits

You have great endurance, tenacity, and self-control, and your strong willpower will overcome almost anything. You are very caring and protective toward your family, especially your partner.

Your Bad Bits

You can be secretive, suspicious, inflexible, vindictive, and ruthless.

Your Love and Sex Style

Scorpios are intense, and when you fall in love, your feelings run deep and true. Sex is vital to your health and happiness, and you can take this to extremes when the mood hits you.

Your Weaknesses

You are prone to self-destruction, violence, moodiness, and clannishness.

Your Food and Drink Weaknesses

You love to eat and you may occasionally overdo it where sweet foods and chocolate are concerned. Most of you hate to be out of control, so when you use alcohol, it is usually in moderation.

Your Best Day
Tuesday: traditionally assigned to the Roman god Mars, your sign's ancient ruler.

Your Worst Day
Friday.

Your Colors
Dark red, dark purple.

Your Cities
Brisbane, Liverpool, Milwaukee, New Orleans, Washington DC.

Your Countries
Brazil, Norway, Syria, Zimbabwe.

Your Vacations
You are too restless to sit on a beach for long. A sea cruise probably appeals because you love the sea and you enjoy waking up in new places every day.

Your Landscapes
You love being on or by the sea and by lakes and rivers. You also enjoy high places or hot and humid areas. Many Scorpios love deserts.

Your Foods
Scorpios are supposed to like hot and spicy foods but you tend to have a delicate stomach, so you prefer plain and ordinary foods like fish or meat and two vegetables. Fried food upsets you. Traditional astrology suggests peppers and leeks. We suggest that you hold the peppers and go for the leeks instead.

Your Herbs
Basil.

Your Tissue Salts
Ferrous phosphate, calcium sulfate, calcium phosphate.

Your Aromatherapy Essence
Ylang-ylang.

Your Bach Flower Remedy
Impatiens.

Your Trees
Blackthorn, hawthorn, any thorny bush or tree, possibly something like acacia.

Your Flowers
Rhododendron, dark red flowers, also cacti.

Your Animals
Scorpion, eagle, shark, mule, and snake.

Your Metal
Iron is associated with Mars, the ancient ruler of Scorpio. Iron has a low melting point and it oxidizes to a reddish color. These days, plutonium has been added as a Scorpio metal, but it isn't recommended to wear this as jewelry!

Your Gems
Opal, obsidian, onyx, jet, marcasite.

Your Mode of Dress
You love to shock, so you could turn up looking like Cher in one of her more outrageous outfits. Otherwise, both

sexes like wearing casual clothes such as jeans and colorful shirts.

Your Careers

You need a meaningful job, so you may go in for some form of teaching, training, or counseling. Many Scorpios work in the medical field, especially as surgeons, but some join the police or get involved with post mortem and forensic work. Other traditionally Scorpio careers are psychiatrist, butcher, miner, and engineer.

Your Friends

People who are not afraid of you and who are as passionate about life as you are.

Your Enemies

You have contempt for timid people, and you may be uncomfortable around aloof and pretentious people.

Your Attitude to Money

Your moods control the way you spend or save money at any one point in time and this can make you difficult to understand and to live with. You can go through periods of the most amazing parsimony and then spend money as though it is going out of fashion.

Your Favorite Automobile

You need a big, fast, powerful automatic limo with tinted windows and plenty of gadgets in it. An ejector seat for irritating passengers would be nice.

Your Ideal Home

You would go crazy in a small apartment, because you need space and the sight of trees, fields, and landscapes. You need room for your hobbies and interests and for all your books.

Your Preferred Drink

Scorpios either drink a great deal or practically nothing at all. Many of you enjoy whisky, especially the many different kinds of malts.

Your Favorite Meal Out

Your stomach is sensitive, so spicy foods and anything that is unfamiliar is not liked. Many Scorpios enjoy eating soup, either the thin kind with a little pasta added or a thick country broth.

Your Night Out

Some male Scorpios enjoy lap dancing or strip clubs while others prefer something more refined such as a concert, musical, or a pop concert. You love to entertain friends and family in a pub, club, or restaurant.

Your Preferred Activities

You love to travel, but you also enjoy spending money on indulgent things that you can't normally afford. This could include CDs, or spending time luxuriating in a health spa. Many of you also enjoy swimming, diving, and playing team sports and games.

Your Favorite Television Program

You enjoy watching any kind of sport, including car racing. Documentary programs appeal; also adventures and all those detective programs.

The Gift You Would Most Appreciate

You hate anything that is cheap and nasty so any gift, however small should be of the highest quality. You love music so a couple of CDs or tickets to a musical or pop event would delight you. Nice clothes or something attractive for the home always goes down well, as does aftershave, perfume, or good jewelry. Scorpio men love knives, so a clever Swiss army knife or a real killer of a flick knife would be appreciated. (As long as you don't get arrested before you have handed it over!) Sports or photographic equipment is also liked.

The Books You Enjoy
Factual and history books, especially about wars and exciting times; spy stories, thrillers, and novels with an occult theme.

The Music You Enjoy
Classical, some pop, also country and western music.

The Games and Sports That You Enjoy
You love to watch or play tough sports such as rugby, American football, soccer, rough team games, boxing, swimming, fencing, shooting, and fishing. In short, anything where you can really stretch your body, bludgeon others, or try to kill something!

Your Potential Health Problems
The sexual organs, the stomach and digestive system, lower spine, groin, blood disorders, eye problems, squints, and so on. There can be sudden unexplained paralysis.

Your Lucky Number
Eight.

Your Money Luck
Mainly you earn what you need, and you may also provide for others, but you can inherit money, property, or goods from other family members.

Your Karmic Lesson
Your role is to cope with partners in private and business life and to care for the needs of weak people or animals.

Success in Love and Compatibility

Scorpio with Aries
An extremely hot sexual union, but there would also be many arguments, as each tries to dominate the other. You would soon resort to emotional blackmail to get your own way.

Scorpio with Taurus
Shared interests can make this a good combination as long as you are in the market for a settled relationship, otherwise you might find Taurus too quiet for your taste and you could become bored and restless in the long run.

Scorpio with Gemini
You both like to talk and discuss things, so this would work well as a friendship, but as a long-term love relationship, you would dominate Gemini, making your partner depressed and unhappy.

Scorpio with Cancer
You both act on gut feelings rather than logic, and that is fine as long as you are both singing the same song; otherwise you could find yourselves out of tune.

Scorpio with Leo
This either works very well or not at all. At best, both of you are playful and love a bit of drama and fun in life. Sexually, this could be great fun but it may not work out in the long run.

Scorpio with Virgo
Both of you are extremely critical, and you are both touchy. You could end up resenting each other, which is not a good prospect for a long-term relationship.

Scorpio with Libra

You need a partner who will make a deep and abiding commitment to the relationship, and Libra finds that extremely difficult. Your arguments could be memorable, but the long-term outlook is not good.

Scorpio with Scorpio

This would either be a marriage made in heaven or one that ends in hell! It might be fun in the short term, but you are too alike for comfort.

Scorpio with Sagittarius

You are so different in your approach to life that it would be a difficult match. Sagittarius needs to be free, whereas you can be possessive.

Scorpio with Capricorn

Capricorn likes to make decisions, and as long as they are sensible ones, you will go along with them most of the time. Capricorn can stand up to you, so it could work well for both of you.

Scorpio with Aquarius

Both signs are extremely obstinate and tense, so this would very likely become a real battleground. Furthermore, you take decisions as a result of gut feeling, while Aquarius is logical and long-winded.

Scorpio with Pisces

Both are emotional and intuitive, so as long as you have plenty of shared interests, you can get along very well. You may have to take most of the responsibility in this relationship, as Pisces often needs practical help.

9

All You Want to Know About
Sagittarius

Your Element—Fire

Fire signs are called the initiators of the zodiac because they don't allow grass to grow under their feet. If a job needs to be done, no one can do it more quickly and effectively than you. However, if the job is a long-winded one that requires persistence, you may have to find someone else to come in and finish it for you. You grasp opportunities when they are offered, and you don't understand those who do not have the courage and initiative to do the same themselves. Your intelligence and courage are to be admired, but you can become arrogant and overbearing with those whom you consider less able than yourself. You are a spendthrift, but you are as likely to spend money on others as on yourself.

Your Quality—Mutable

You are able to adapt fairly easily to new circumstances, and you appreciate a change of scenery from time to time. You don't have a very strong personality, so you are happiest when living and working with people who nurture you and make you feel good about yourself. You love your family, but you occasionally need to get away and spend a little time alone in order to recharge your emotional batteries.

Your Ruling Planet—Jupiter

Jupiter (Jove) was the king of the Roman gods. He was jolly and jovial most of the time, but when he was in a temper he hurled thunderbolts down on those who angered him.

Your Symbol—the Archer or the Centaur

The king of the centaurs was a noted archer called Chiron. He taught the Greek heroes Hercules, Theseus, and Jason not only how to shoot straight, but also how to heal. Jupiter placed Chiron among the stars after an accident in which he was wounded and unable to heal himself.

Your Appearance

Although there are small Sagittarians, you are probably tall and well built, even a little on the heavy side. Your body is out of proportion, either with large arms and chest and a slim lower half or a small top and large hips and thighs.

Your Part of the Body

Sagittarius rules the hips and thighs and the circulation through the legs.

Your Good Bits

You have a wonderful sense of humor, and you are intelligent, honest, and optimistic. Your values are spiritual rather than materialistic.

Your Bad Bits

You can be tactless, unrealistic, and blind to the truth where it concerns yourself. You also talk about doing things without actually getting around to them or barge ahead and get into a muddle.

Your Love and Sex Style

You need freedom within a relationship or to be free of permanent ties altogether, and chances are that you are a better friend than you are a partner. Sexually you are probably ready to try anything once—or more than once if possible. Some Sagittarians are far more conventional in their attitudes to both love and sex.

Your Weaknesses

Traveling, making new friends, and forgetting your old ones.

Your Food and Drink Weaknesses

You love wine, and you may overdo your consumption from time to time. You may enjoy trying exotic or ethnic foods and fast food. Alternatively, you can be a fussy eater, only able to cope with a small range of foods.

Your Best Day

Thursday: associated with the Roman god Jupiter.

Your Worst Day

Saturday.

Your Colors

Royal blue and imperial purple.

Your Cities

Archangel, Bradford (USA), Budapest, Cologne, Dallas, Haines (Canada), Toledo, Tucson, Wellington.

Your Countries

Australia, Hungary, Madagascar, the "cowboy country" in the west of the USA.

Your Vacations

You are the great explorer of the zodiac, so you may want to climb remote mountains or journey up the Orinoco. If not, you would enjoy a sporty holiday that allows you to play golf, windsurf, ski, ride horses, or try your hand at parasailing. Some Sagittarians appreciate nothing more exciting than a deck chair and a good book.

Your Landscapes

Farming areas where horses and cattle are kept, in addition to open moorland.

Your Foods

Traditional astrology suggests that you like fruit, currents, asparagus, and tomatoes. You probably eat most things but sugar or acid foods seem to upset you.

Your Herbs

Aniseed.

Your Tissue Salts

Ferrous phosphate, sodium sulfate, silica.

Your Aromatherapy Essence

Rosemary.

Your Bach Flower Remedy

Vervain.

Your Trees

Oak, lime, mulberry, ash, and birch.

Your Flowers

Dandelion, pinks, rushes, and the pimpernel.

Your Animals

Sheep, stag, elephant, tiger, and horse.

Your Metal

Tin.

Your Gems

There are various gems associated with your sign, including the topaz, carbuncle, and sapphire.

Your Mode of Dress

You prefer casual clothes for everyday life and really eccentric outfits when you feel like dressing up. You may choose to wear everything in one strange color, such as mauve or orange.

Your Careers

Many Sagittarians float around for years until they find the right niche. Most love to teach, write, and broadcast, so there are many Sagittarians in the media. Your strongly spiritual side can lead you into a religious organization or into spiritualism and spirit healing. You could also work as a publisher or a lawyer or in some aspect of the travel trade, even as a safari guide.

Your Friends

They must have a sense of humor and not be too critical.

Your Enemies

You cannot stand pretentious or very serious people or those who use their intelligence to take advantage of others.

Your Attitude to Money

How you get by is a mystery to us all! You studiously avoid doing anything the least bit sensible with your money, but you have the luck of the Irish when it comes to winning money, marrying it, or just finding it when you most need it.

Your Favorite Automobile

You are happy with anything that gets you from A to B. You may drive about in something large and scruffy that has plenty of character, like an old pickup truck or an old van that has been customized with your favorite spray-paint can. A motorcycle may suit your needs.

Your Ideal Home

You prefer a home in the country where there is plenty of space around you; if it is near water, so much the better. You also need to be able to get into town to visit interesting shops from time to time. You need space for your hobbies and your collection of interesting odds and ends.

Your Preferred Drink

You probably quaff large quantities of wine or ale until your stomach or liver start to complain.

Your Favorite Meal Out

You either like exotic and interesting food or something bland, such as pasta, or a traditional kind of meal.

Your Night Out

Anything that has a sporting or competitive element would suit you, so you might go to a basketball game, a boxing match, or you may take your friends skating.

Your Preferred Activities

Fishing, swimming, exploring, and wandering around the shops.

Your Favorite Television Program

Your attention span is so short that you probably only concentrate on the commercials! You prefer to be out than at home watching the tube.

The Gift You Would Most Appreciate

You have an offbeat sense of humor so you appreciate anything that is quirky or different. An interesting ornament that reflects your special interests would please you. If you are able to care for a pet, you might appreciate a tank full of tropical fish or a pet snake!

Otherwise, a backpack, wheeled luggage, dramatic jewelry, or a garish sweater covered in sequins!

The Books You Enjoy

Tourist guides to exotic places. Factual books on spiritual or out-of-the ordinary matters. You also enjoy fantasy and science fiction.

The Music You Enjoy

Amusing music with funny lyrics appeals to you. Otherwise pretty standard pop and rock music and country and western tunes.

The Games and Sports That You Enjoy

Sagittarians are supposed to love the outdoor life and to be especially interested in horse riding or horse racing. This may not necessarily be so, but you would enjoy team games or golf, tennis, or archery in a nice country club atmosphere. If in town, you might enjoy squash or aerobics in an expensive leisure center.

Your Potential Health Problems

Your weak spots are your hips and thighs and the circulation through the legs. Your liver, pituitary gland and some parts of the circulatory system may be sensitive.

Your Lucky Number
Nine.

Your Money Luck

Nobody is luckier than a Sagittarian, so you can expect more than a few windfalls in your life or wins on raffles, lotteries, and so on.

Your Karmic Lesson

Your job seems to be to learn through some form of suffering and to allow your soul to grow so that you can have a better incarnation the next time around.

Success in Love and Compatibility

Sagittarius with Aries

You both do everything at the speed of light, so you don't irritate each other. You need more patience than Aries can muster, although you would become good friends.

Sagittarius with Taurus

You have so little in common that it is hard to see how you could stay interested in each other over the long term. An initial attraction of opposites might make for a pleasant fling though.

Sagittarius with Gemini

You share a great sense of humor and a desire to get out and about and see new people and places. You enjoy each other's company and share many interests, so this could be a successful relationship.

Sagittarius with Cancer

Cancer loves home life and to have the family, parents, children, and in-laws around, while you need freedom, space and time to think. We can't see this working in the long run.

Sagittarius with Leo

Competitiveness and arguments could mar an otherwise good match, but a short fling or a friendship might work, even though a long-term relationship would be hard to maintain.

Sagittarius with Virgo

You share a great sense of humor, but Virgo values hard work while you prefer an easy life, so you may have to accept that one of you will earn the bread and butter for both of you.

Sagittarius with Libra

Both of you live in dreamland half the time, so as long as you can earn enough to keep the home from falling apart, you can drift and dream together.

Sagittarius with Scorpio

Scorpio is possessive and far too interested in what is going on in your mind for comfort. You share an interest in travel, so as friends you can get on quite well together, for a while at least.

Sagittarius with Sagittarius

You either get on famously together, or you soon find yourselves becoming irritated by your similarities. Neither of you like long term relationships much, so it may not last.

Sagittarius with Capricorn

You could find Capricorn's ambition hard to cope with but as long as you allow your partner to get on with earning the money while you plan trips and outings it could work.

Sagittarius with Aquarius

You are both independent and intelligent so you would certainly become good friends. Your shared interest in sexual experimentation could help to cement the relationship.

Sagittarius with Pisces

This could be an extremely successful relationship if you happen to share spiritual interests. If you don't, then you won't have enough in common deep down, where it really matters.

10

All You Want to Know About
Capricorn

r Element—Earth

diligent, hardworking, and are often
ıg something useful. You can be relied
it might take you a while to get around
: thorough and capable, but you cannot
assed or rushed. You have a creative
streak anu ⌐ ___ sensuality means that you know how to
make things (and people) look and feel good.

Being shrewd and cautious, you need material and
emotional security, and you will put up with a lot in order
to get it and keep it. You may appear stingy to outsiders,
but this is because you fear poverty. You cling to your
family, but being sociable, you don't usually keep
outsiders at a distance.

Your Quality—Cardinal

There is a kind of self-centeredness about all cardinal
sign people, which means it is hard to push you into
doing things you don't want to do. You're able to come up
with some great ideas, but you may not always be able to
carry them out. You take responsibility easily, and you
care for those who are weaker than yourself, but if others
try to hold you back, you will resist.

Your Ruling Planet—Saturn

This rather gloomy Roman god represents limitations
and hard lessons in life, but the musical and cheerful god
Pan is also associated with Capricorn.

Your Symbol—the Goat

This sign is said to represent the mythical goat Amalthea,
who suckled Jupiter in his infancy. Playfully, the baby
god pulled off one of her horns, which then became the
Cornucopia, or horn of plenty. The merry, goat-footed
god Pan is also associated with this sign. The mountain

goat climbs onward and upward in a sure-footed Capricorn manner.

Your Appearance

You are most likely slim and of medium height. Your bone structure is good and this will stand you in good stead when you get older; indeed, you may look old when you are young and young when you are old.

Your Part of the Body

Capricorn rules the skin, ears, bones, knees, and teeth. This sign is also associated with chronic ailments such as rheumatism.

Your Good Bits

You work hard, look after your family, and you have a sense of duty. You also have a good sense of humor and you can be sociable and great fun when you are in the right mood. You are realistic.

Your Bad Bits

You can be dull and dry, stingy, and lacking in imagination.

Your Love and Sex Style

You are cautious about the people you choose to love, and you don't like to move from one partner to another. You may reserve most of your love for your parents and other family members. Sexually you can be slightly experimental, but for the most part you prefer to stick to the tried and tested.

Your Weaknesses

You are ambitious, and as long as this is kept in proportion, it is all well and good; however, you may forget the needs of those around you. You like status symbols and a comfortable lifestyle, but you are prepared to work for this. You may be stingy and also prone to depression.

Your Food and Drink Weaknesses
You may overdo the junk food and snacks or even go without food at times when your heavy workload makes it impossible for you to eat properly. Your sign is not noted for drinking much alcohol, but you like a shot of whisky or a cocktail with friends as a pleasant interlude.

Your Best Day
Saturday. This is the day associated with the Roman god Saturn. Literally, Saturn's day.

Your Worst Day
Thursday.

Your Colors
Black, gray, dark green, mustard, and brown.

Your Cities
Brussels, Delhi, Hartford, Mexico City, Rio de Janeiro, Saint John (Canada).

Your Countries
Afghanistan, the Balkans, India, Lithuania, Mexico, the West Indies.

Your Vacations
You are fond of traveling, and you like to take some fairly gentle exercise. Therefore, a holiday by the sea, offering an opportunity to go sailing or walking, might suit you.

Your Landscapes
High mountains (remember the symbol of the goat), rock, and snow.

Your Foods
You were probably taught to eat up your dinner and not to waste food when you were small. You probably still eat more or less what is put in front of you, and you are unlikely to be a fussy eater.

Your Herbs
Sage and sorrel.

Your Tissue Salts
Calcium phosphate, silica, potassium chloride.

Your Aromatherapy Essence
Coriander.

Your Bach Flower Remedy
Elm.

Your Trees
Yew.

Your Flowers
Pansy, hemlock, ivy, and thistle.

Your Animals
Goat, donkey, elephant, and toad.

Your Metal
Lead.

Your Gems

There are a number of gems associated with your sign,
including the turquoise, black opal, and tourmaline.

Your Mode of Dress

When young, you prefer fairly formal clothes of good
quality that are made to last. When you get older, you
become a bit more adventurous and are happy to try out
different colors and styles.

Your Careers

You are attuned to a professional career, with
accountancy and banking being high on the list.
However, any kind of large business would attract you,
especially if the job included detailed work and didn't
require you to be hurried. You may also choose to be a
dentist, doctor, lawyer, or property dealer. Yours is the
scientific sign, so some form of scientific research or
collation of evidence might suit you.

Your Friends

You respect people who are loyal, hardworking, and fair,
but you are closest to your family, and friends come a
long way behind them.

Your Enemies

You can't tolerate feckless or stupid people who ignore
authority.

Your Attitude to Money

Being stone broke is just not your style. The chances are
that your parents didn't have much to spare, and you
learned to be sensible, to work hard for your money, and
then to conserve what you have. Take care that your fear
of poverty doesn't turn you into a miser.

Your Favorite Automobile

You would probably enjoy owning some kind of all-weather and all-terrain vehicle, such as a Jeep or a British Land Rover. You probably complain about the running costs. Otherwise an executive limo would suit you.

Your Ideal Home

If possible, you would choose to live in a warm country or in a home with excellent central heating. You can live in a flat, but you need to get out of it as often as possible to indulge in your hobbies and interests. You would prefer to have your family fairly close by and also to have them drop in on you as often as possible. You would be luckiest when living high up on a hill or a mountain.

Your Preferred Drink

You probably don't like wasting money on alcohol, but when you do drink, you probably prefer a small glass of brandy, a quality wine, or a liqueur.

Your Favorite Meal Out

Capricorns enjoy good food well cooked and presented and at a reasonable price. You may enjoy curries and spicy foods.

Your Night Out

You love to dance and you enjoy upbeat music, so you might like ballroom dancing, old time dancing, line dancing, Latin American dancing or anything else of the kind. You may even enter competitions and become quite professional. Other outings would include picnics and music-in-the-park type of events.

Your Preferred Activities

You probably like to work as much as anything else, but you can be equally happy decorating your house. When you do relax, it will be by doing things with your family or playing with your pets.

Your Favorite Television Program

You probably enjoy collecting your favorite programs on video; otherwise, you have no special favorites, although you may enjoy the soaps.

The Gift You Would Most Appreciate

A computer or some office machinery might please you, as would tools or a musical instrument. You may find it hard to indulge yourself, so anything that is utterly luxurious would suit you. A smart briefcase or desk set might suit males while nice clothes or a trip to the beautician's would please the ladies. A night out with dinner and dancing on the menu would be nice too. You would appreciate a nice clock or watch, monogrammed stationery, CDs, a pair of hiking boots, or an electronic organizer.

The Books You Enjoy

You enjoy reading novels that give you something to think about and to discuss with your partner; you also like newspapers and specialist magazines.

The Music You Enjoy

You may like the blues, classical music, or music that you can dance to.

The Games and Sports That You Enjoy

Many Capricorns love to dance; you may also enjoy climbing. Team games are not really your thing. Board games that have a mathematic, financial, or strategic element to them may please you—Monopoly for example.

Your Potential Health Problems

The knees are especially vulnerable, as are the bones and skin, ears, and teeth. You may suffer from problems associated with the gallbladder, digestion, and the spleen. Capricorn is associated with chronic ailments such as rheumatism, asthma, and eczema.

Your Lucky Number
Ten.

Your Money Luck

You work for what you get, and sometimes it is a long time coming. You have better luck in old age than when you are young.

Your Karmic Lesson

You will always work hard and look after your family and close friends. You may be too dutiful and austere, so you should learn to lighten up.

Success in Love and Compatibility

Capricorn with Aries

Both of you are capable, hardworking, and ambitious, and while your partner is politically adroit, you have common sense. As long as you have a shared goal, you can enjoy an amazingly happy and productive life together.

Capricorn with Taurus
You understand each other's needs and priorities, and you go at the same pace as each other, so this can be a perfect match.

Capricorn with Gemini
About the only things you have in common are fussiness and a tendency to martyr yourselves for your families. An unusual but occasionally successful union.

Capricorn with Cancer
Your attitudes to family life, money, and business are extremely similar, so you can make a real go of this. However, it works best when Cancer is the homemaker and Capricorn the worker.

Capricorn with Leo
This would be an extremely competitive partnership with both of you striving to be the boss. You would respond by trying to restrict Leo in some way, and this is one battle that you would lose even before you started.

Capricorn with Virgo
You see life from similar points of view and you share many points of nature in common. As long as you don't both sink into dullness and depression, you can have a comfortable and happy life together.

Capricorn with Libra
Some Capricorns are sociable and outgoing; if you are one of these, you and your Libran partner would have a lot of fun together. You will be happy to work hard while Libra spends money so elegantly.

Capricorn with Scorpio
There is no reason on earth why this should work, but it often does. It is as if you each supply the missing parts of each other's natures, and Scorpio will help you to achieve your ambitions.

Capricorn with Sagittarius
This would be a difficult love relationship, but possibly a happy working one, as Sagittarius would bring enthusiasm to the venture.

Capricorn with Capricorn
Not all Capricorns are alike, but your basic beliefs and priorities will be the same, so there will be enough in common and enough that is different to create some kind of spark. If you are too alike though, the spark will be too feeble to last.

Capricorn with Aquarius
Aquarius suffers from foot-in-mouth syndrome and you take offense over everything, so after an initial period of attraction, you would soon fall out.

Capricorn with Pisces
You are dutiful and organized while Pisces is intuitive, romantic, fond of mysticism, and totally disorganized, so this might be an interesting short-term affair for you both, but it won't stand the test of time.

11

All You Want to Know About
Aquarius

Your Element—Air

Yours is the element of communication, so you will always choose a job and a lifestyle that keeps you in touch with others and that takes you from place to place. You need a variety of interests in your life, with plenty of places to go and people to see. You may spend more time on the phone than is healthy for your bank balance, but talking to others keeps you sane, so what the heck! Your mind is quick, and you can often see solutions to other people's problems, although you are less able to solve your own problems when they arise.

Your Quality—Fixed

Your fixed nature means that it takes you a while before you find the right partner, the right job, or the right place to live, but once you have, you stick to your choices. Sometimes you hang on to things when it would be better to let them go; this can bring you pain in the long run. You are thorough, and you can finish all that you start.

Your Ruling Planet—Uranus

This planet behaves very different from all the others in the solar system as its poles are at its east and west and it revolves in a different direction from all the other planets. Therefore, astrologers believe that it represents unpredictable behavior and eccentricity. Before the discovery of Uranus, Saturn was considered to be the ruler of Aquarius.

Your Symbol—the Water Carrier

This confuses beginners in astrology, as they invariably link the Water Carrier symbol to the element of water, but as we have already seen, Aquarius is actually an air sign. The Water Carrier represents a reservoir of knowledge. Other aspects of this deep symbol include a cloud of water carried through the air. This is a frightening symbol for people born during the twentieth century because it carries images of nuclear fallout and of course, uranium is associated with Aquarius.

Your Appearance

Most Aquarians are average to tall in height and they have a high forehead, which is accentuated in men because their hairline often recedes fairly early in life. The eyes are often quite magnetic, the expression is serious, and they speak slowly. Other Aquarians are short and overweight, with thick wavy hair, and they are altogether quicker in everything than the other type.

Your Part of the Body

Aquarius rules the ankles, circulation to the extremities, and breathing.

Your Good Bits

You are friendly, independent, and talented, and you have an excellent mind.

Your Bad Bits

It is hard for you to get in touch with your own emotions. You rebel against authority and you can be as eccentric and as vague as an absent-minded professor.

Your Love and Sex Style

Some Aquarians are too independent to stay with anyone for long, while others marry young and stay put. If you fall in love, your feelings run deep and you are serious about marriage; if you don't, you can be amazingly casual about the feelings of others. Sex is very important to your sign and you are a generous and inventive lover.

Your Weaknesses

Your ability to argue logically and endlessly would impress Mr. Spock or any other Vulcan.

Your Food and Drink Weaknesses

You are not a fussy eater, and you like a wide range of foods, but you particularly enjoy tasty dishes such as Chinese or Thai foods. You also love salty snacks, olives, and pickles, as well as cookies and fruitcake. You need to watch your salt and sugar intake as these can cause an imbalance.

Your Best Day

Saturday. Before the planet Uranus was discovered, your ruling planet was Saturn, and Saturday is Saturn's day.

Your Worst Day
Monday.

Your Colors
Neon colors, electric blue, lilac, violet, purple, and indigo.

Your Cities
Bremen, Brighton, Dayton, Halifax (Canada), Hamburg, Lubbock, Miami, Moscow, Salisbury, Toronto.

Your Countries
Ethiopia, Russia, Sweden.

Your Vacations

You like places that are interesting and that offer good quality food and accommodations. You would probably enjoy a visit to the Kennedy Space Center in Florida.

Aquarians cannot really be categorized, but generally speaking you are not great travelers.

Your Landscapes

You enjoy natural, uncultivated places and open, hilly areas with good views and wonderful light. You also love to be by the sea.

Your Foods

Most Aquarians are pretty easy to cater to but some are vegetarian due to a dislike of killing and eating animals. Some can be faddish in other ways.

Your Herbs

Your sign is probably more attuned to spices like cumin than to herbs, but fennel is associated with Aquarius.

Your Tissue Salts

Sodium chloride, ferrous phosphate, potassium phosphate.

Your Aromatherapy Essence

Cypress.

Your Bach Flower Remedy.

Sweet chestnut.

Your Trees

Willow.

Your Flowers

Orchids, absinthe, buttercup.

Your Animals

Cat, hare, mouse.

Your Metal

These days uranium is considered to be the metal for your sign, but lead was the metal that was associated with Saturn, the old ruler of Aquarius. Platinum is also considered to be an Aquarian metal.

Your Gems

There are two gems associated with your sign; lapis lazuli and amethyst. Many Aquarians enjoy buying crystals for meditation or healing purposes.

Your Mode of Dress

Aquarians are so individual that it is impossible to categorize you, but one thing that seems to be shared by all of you is a dislike of wearing suits. You may choose clothes that are stylish, casual, or totally individual and quite eccentric. You hate fussy and formal clothes.

Your Careers

You like to help people, and you have a friendly, non-judgmental attitude, so you can be a teacher, an advisor, an arbitrator, or a lawyer. In addition, you like new technology, so you may go in for computer science, rocketry, or some other branch of scientific exploration. Your idealism can lead to a career in a charity organization, but you may also take up astrology or counseling.

Your Friends

You need plenty of friends, and they must be clever, kind, interesting, and humorous.

Your Enemies

You dislike overly emotional people who want to cling and drain you.

Your Attitude to Money

Eccentric to the last, your attitude to finances defies all understanding. You know exactly what you should do to save money, but somehow the theory doesn't always translate into practice—especially when a new gadget comes onto the market!

Your Favorite Automobile

You like a large vehicle with a good engine and plenty of power. You may enjoy a digital dashboard and a computerized illustration of the inside and outside temperature, a moving map, a radar detector, and a wonderful sound system. This space-age machine will either be kept in a pristine state or it will be utterly filthy. You love to have space for all your goods, so a minivan would appeal as well.

Your Ideal Home

Aquarians are so peculiar that it is hard to say how you would choose to live. Some of you like a home full of animals, children, noise, and mess and others need a spare, cool-looking home with loads of space. Some love soft, feminine colors, while others would enjoy living with stark, modernistic black-and-white furnishings. Many of you love the idea of living in an old castle or some other ancient pile that is filled with loads of antiques and interesting junk.

Your Preferred Drink

You enjoy talking over a drink and a meal with friends, so plenty of red wine, beer, lager, or any other type of social drink is acceptable, but you rarely drink to excess.

Your Favorite Meal Out

You may be a vegetarian or a "funny" eater. If not, you enjoy experimenting with ethnic cuisine such as Chinese,

Jewish, Italian, Greek, Lebanese, vegetarian, Oriental or any kind of specialized food.

Your Night Out

Your sign is so unpredictable and so interested in things that are a bit different that you could enjoy a fireworks display and an evening at a fairground, complete with a hot dog and mustard. Alternatively, you may love to pamper yourself at a spa, go to an astrology workshop, or attend a poetry reading.

Your Preferred Activities

You enjoy playing gentle sports, chatting with friends, having a Tarot reading, or losing yourself in a book.

Your Favorite Television Program

Cartoons, science fiction—you may even be a Trekkie or, if British, a "Doctor Who" fan. Documentaries and educational programs are liked, as are interesting plays and murder mysteries or spy stories.

The Gift You Would Most Appreciate

You may be eccentric, but you do appreciate a touch of luxury. Therefore a good-quality gift that reflects your special interest would suit you. You may collect china animals, chess sets, Japanese tea sets, or Tarot cards, so an addition to your collection would be nice. Another idea would be a reading with a good astrologer. Otherwise you enjoy bookshelves and plenty of books to put on them, electronic gadgets, and anything to do with computers.

The Books You Enjoy

Owning books is as important to you as reading them , and you encourage your family to do the same. You love to be surrounded by books, newspapers, magazines, pamphlets, and bits of paper with writing on them. To do you justice however, you do try to read everything within your reach and will even read the advertising on a packet of cereal rather than have nothing for your eyes to wander over. Many Aquarians enjoy science fiction and books about interesting and outlandish things such as UFOs.

The Music You Enjoy

This could be anything from classical to rock music, but you don't much care for background "Muzak." Some of you love jazz or clever synthesizer music, while others are keen on new-age music, the sound of a sitar, or something equally unusual.

The Games and Sports That You Enjoy

Word games such as Scrabble and also chess. You probably don't enjoy team games, but golf may appeal, or anything that you can do alone, such as fishing. Many Aquarians like tap or ballroom dancing. Some of you prefer attending interesting seminars (especially astrology ones) and committee meetings to any kind of games or sports.

Your Potential Health Problems

Your weak points are the ankles and circulation to the extremities, and your breathing. This sign is also associated with cramps and nervous breakdowns.

Your Lucky Number
Eleven.

Your Money Luck

You are fairly sensible where money is concerned, so you will work, save, set up a pension scheme, and spend as little as necessary most of the time. You can be lucky with property dealings, especially if you are one of the many Aquarians who likes doing renovations and decorating and then selling or renting out property.

Your Karmic Lesson

You have to learn to get close to others and to avoid becoming isolated. Another lesson is to learn and then to teach and advise others.

Success in Love and Compatibility

Aquarius with Aries

You can dream up good ideas, while Aries can get things off the ground. You don't object to Aries flirtatiousness either, so you can get along very well together.

Aquarius with Taurus

You are both obstinate and unlikely to see the other's point of view unless you both learn to give way from time to time. You respect Taurus's practicality.

Aquarius with Gemini

Gemini is better at working and earning money than you are. In addition, you share an interest in sex, so you could have a successful and exciting relationship.

Aquarius with Cancer

Cancer's clingy nature doesn't fit well with your need for independence. You don't think alike, because you are logical while Cancer jumps to conclusions or acts on intuition and instinct.

Aquarius with Leo

You can be inspired by Leo, and you can be friends who respect one another as well as being lovers. You are both interested in lovemaking, so this also helps the relationship along.

Aquarius with Virgo
This can just work, as long as Virgo doesn't need too much reassurance and is not too fussy and neurotic. You share a wonderful sense of fun and sense of humor.

Aquarius with Libra
This can be a good combination as long as neither of you is the argumentative type. You share intellectual interests but you may not share Libra's interest in art and homemaking.

Aquarius with Scorpio
You are both stubborn, and you both tend to think that you are right all the time, so this is not a good match. Scorpio's emotional approach to life will confuse you.

Aquarius with Sagittarius
This is a fun combination with many shared interests, but you are both independent and neither of you may be in a hurry to make a long-term commitment.

Aquarius with Capricorn
You have some interests in common, but you are idealistic while Capricorn is status-conscious and materialistic, so you could clash.

Aquarius with Aquarius
There is such variation from one Aquarian to the next that you are all different from each other! This keeps boredom at bay.

Aquarius with Pisces

Anything can happen in this weird and wonderful match, as you are both idealists, but you are both impractical so you would need a good accountant to help run your lives.

12

All You Want to Know About Pisces

Your Element—Water

This is the element of emotion, and you are certainly sensitive and emotional. Your feelings run deep, and you tend to let your emotions spill over into areas of your life where logic would serve you better. You often make decisions on the spur of the moment based on your feelings at the time, but that you regret later in life.

Your Quality—Mutable

You are able to adapt fairly easily to new circumstances, and you appreciate a change of scenery from time to time. You don't have a very strong personality, so you are happiest when living and working with people who nurture you and make you feel good about yourself. You love your family, but you occasionally need to get away and spend a little time alone in order to recharge your emotional batteries.

Your Ruling Planet—Neptune

The Roman god Neptune ruled the sea and all the mysterious things that are hidden from sight under it. Before the planet Neptune was discovered, your sign was said to be ruled by Jupiter.

Your Symbol—the Fish

Two fish that are tied together and swimming in different directions are the symbol for your sign. The Babylonians knew the constellation of Pisces as "Kun," which means "the tails." This is very appropriate for the last sign of the zodiac. It was also known as "the leash," which was the link between the two fish. The symbol itself may commemorate the occasion when Venus and Cupid disguised themselves as fish in order to escape from an angry giant.

Your Appearance

You are of middling height and weight or are a little on the tall side; you can gain weight later in life. You have a lovely smile and eyes that light up when you laugh. Unfortunately, your features suffer from the weather and from aging, so you need to use plenty of good products on your face and may even need to resort to plastic surgery later in life.

Your Part of the Body

Your sign rules the feet, the mind, and the psychic and intuitive faculties. It also rules the lungs.

Your Good Bits

You are imaginative, sensitive, creative, and helpful to those who are in pain or difficulty.

Your Bad Bits

You can be indecisive, inclined to worry over nothing, and you find it hard to finish what you start.

Your Love and Sex Style

You can be happy in a loving relationship as long as you have the space to be yourself. If someone gives you the third degree about where you are going and what time you will be back, it will drive you insane. Sexually, you are prepared to try most things—especially when you have had a few drinks!

Your Weaknesses

You can muddle along in a chaotic state, avoid making decisions, and sink into escapism by drinking alcohol and taking drugs.

Your Food and Drink Weaknesses

You love to cook and eat, and you are not a picky eater, although the animal lovers among you may opt for a vegetarian diet. Alcohol is your real downfall.

Your Best Day

Thursday. The days of the week predate the discovery of the outer planets; therefore your day is Thursday, which is Jupiter's day.

Your Worst Day

Wednesday.

Your Colors

Sea colors, green-blues, turquoise, lavender, lilac, and purple.

Your Cities

Alexandria, Christchurch, Cincinnati, Norfolk (USA), Regina (Canada), San Diego, Sao Paolo, Seville.

Your Countries

New Zealand, Portugal, the Sahara.

Your Vacations

You love to be in, on, or near the sea. You enjoy sea views, and some of you like snorkeling and scuba diving where you can literally be in your element. You would enjoy visiting any area that has a coral reef that you can swim near or look at through a glass-bottomed boat.

Your Landscapes

You appreciate seashores, coastal cliffs, lakes, and fast-moving rivers.

Your Foods

You may be a vegetarian because you may feel that it is wrong to eat the flesh of animals. If you are not too bothered about this, you probably like fish and seafood. You are not a fussy or faddish eater apart from your possible vegetarianism.

Your Herbs

You are more attuned to spices than to herbs; cloves are supposed to link with your sign. However, birthwort, which was supposed to ease the pains of childbirth, is also associated with Pisces.

Your Tissue Salts

Iron phosphate, magnesium phosphate, silica, sodium sulfate.

Your Aromatherapy Essence

Red chestnut.

Your Bach Flower Remedy

Wild rose.

Your Trees

Lime.

Your Flowers

Water lily and poppy. The sign of Pisces is associated with sleep and escapism through drink and narcotics, so the poppy is appropriate. Apart from the modern-day horrors of drug taking, some kinds of poppy have always been used for medicinal purposes.

Your Animals

Fish, dolphin, and the mythical unicorn.

Your Metal
Tin.

Your Gems
There are various gems associated with your sign, including the cool, romantic moonstone, the passionate bloodstone, and the pearl.

Your Mode of Dress
Pisceans simply loved the hippie era and the fancy dress of the Seventies. Nowadays, you probably prefer jeans or casual clothes in gentle, romantic colors. Some of you are very smart and dressy while others wear whatever comes to hand. You are careful with money, so you can do well by trawling thrift and charity shops. Shoes are your weakness—if you overspend, it is on footwear.

Your Careers
Any creative or artistic profession suits you, as does any branch of show business. You love to help others, so you can work for a charity or teach, counsel, or heal people by working in the medical field or by becoming a spiritual healer. There are numerous Piscean Tarot card readers, mediums, healers, psychotherapists, teachers, and astrologers.

Your Friends
You prefer easygoing people who are sympathetic, good listeners, and who have a sense of fun.

Your Enemies
You dislike cold, logical, and heartless people who are cruel to animals or children. You cannot take to formal or fussy types either.

Your Attitude to Money

Your outlook is spiritual rather than materialistic. When you add this to your generosity to your loved ones and your dislike of the rat race, one can see why you rarely have oodles of boodle in the bank.

Your Favorite Automobile

An astonishing number of Pisceans don't drive at all. Others are very fast drivers who love sports vehicles and fast automobiles. In addition to your speedy vehicle, you may have a battered old car or some kind of recreational vehicle.

Your Ideal Home

You would love to live by the sea or some other source of water. You may have a small apartment in town and a house by the sea. Otherwise, anything unusual, such as a converted church or railway station, might suit you. Whatever you choose to live in, there must be a hostelry nearby!

Your Preferred Drink

Anything really! There are even rumors that there is blood in your alcohol!

Your Favorite Meal Out

You are probably a good cook, so you can be fairly discriminating about the standard of food and service when you eat out. Oddly enough, you are more likely to complain about the food in a restaurant than many more apparently assertive people would. Many Pisceans are vegetarians or enjoy fish meals.

Your Night Out

You enjoy a quiz night in a pub or bar and you love to have a drink and chat with friends. Otherwise, a walk by the sea or in pleasant countryside appeals to you. You may enjoy going to a show or to see your favorite sports team play.

Your Preferred Activities
Dreaming, being creative, and using your imagination. Many Pisceans are very good dancers, despite the fact that they are likely to have bad feet.

Your Favorite Television Program
You enjoy biographies, true-life stories, animal and wildlife programs, romance, sagas, and old films of all kinds. You love to laugh, so a good comedy will always go down well with you.

The Gift You Would Most Appreciate
You appreciate art and a touch of luxury. You would love to choose a lovely painting or artistic object and have someone pay for this for you. Otherwise, you may appreciate fishing tackle, some other sports equipment, or a pair of expensive boots.

The Books You Enjoy
You love to read about people, but you also enjoy nonfiction books on your special interest. You read books on natural health therapies and cook books along with newspapers and magazines.

Some of you read about politics or finance, even though you may not involve yourself personally in these things; others read about psychic, fantasy, or mystical subjects.

The Music You Enjoy
You really understand and appreciate music, so whether it is pop or classical, it must be well performed and, if on

CD, the best orchestra and the best quality of recording that you can find.

You might enjoy ballads, ballet music, or something that reminds you of the past. You may like animal-style meditation music with dolphins, birds, and whales singing along to the tune (or lack of tune!).

The Games and Sports That You Enjoy

Oddly enough, Pisceans are quite sporty in various ways. You enjoy walking, aerobics, swimming, and above all, dancing. You love to travel and you may enjoy fishing.

Your Potential Health Problems

Your weak spots are your feet, lungs, and some body fluids. You may suffer from nervous debility, confusion, peculiar mental states, as well as allergic conditions and ailments caused by misuse of drink and drugs

Your Lucky Number
Twelve.

Your Money Luck

Your money fluctuates wildly, and although you are sensible, you can be too generous with your friends and loved ones. You can win lotteries and raffles, but for the most part you need to earn and save if you are to get by. Fortunately, you are one of the workers of the zodiac, so you can always earn money when you need to.

Your Karmic Lesson

You will be called upon to sacrifice something for the sake of others during your lifetime, but you should avoid making a martyr of yourself and allowing others to drain your mental, emotional, and financial resources.

Success in Love and Compatibility

Pisces with Aries

You share some interests and you may get on well enough to make this last. However, Aries could be too pushy for your taste.

Pisces with Taurus

You share an interest in art, music, gardening, the home, and family life. Due to a shared sensual nature and an interest in sex, this relationship can be very good.

Pisces with Gemini

You are both adaptable, and you share a sense of humor, but you may be a little too disorganized for Gemini to cope with in the long term, You could have a pleasant short-term love affair.

Pisces with Cancer

You are both intuitive and both make decisions by instinct rather than by logic, so you have much in common. You both also enjoy family life, homemaking, and travel.

Pisces with Leo

As long as Leo is happy to be the one who earns the money and organizes things, this would work well, as you would take care of the home and the family for your partner.

Pisces with Virgo

With give and take on both sides, this can work well, but you would have to take care not to overburden Virgo. Virgo is happy to take on someone who needs rescuing, but you could rapidly wear out your partner.

Pisces with Libra

You'll have good sexual rapport, but otherwise this could be disappointing, as you both just do not think the same way. You can both dither at times, so you may never get the relationship off the ground.

Pisces with Scorpio

As long as the Scorpio is very loving, this can work well because both of you are emotional, sensitive, and intuitive. If you share an interest in animals, travel, or sex, you would have it made.

Pisces with Sagittarius

You share a great sense of humor and a love of travel, psychic matters, and astrology, so you have much in common. If you can both stand a long-term relationship, this would work.

Pisces with Capricorn

There could be an initial attraction of opposites, but there is so little common ground that this would have very little chance of working out in the long term. Capricorn might be too dull and hardworking for your taste.

Pisces with Aquarius

Neither of you is very practical, but you should get on well in many ways. Aquarius can be stubborn and determined, but you are adaptable—so it could work.

Pisces with Pisces

You both love a drink and a good laugh. You are both pretty easygoing, so as long as there is enough money in the pot, you will be fine together.

13

Differences Within Each Sun Sign

Each sign of the zodiac is divided into three sections that are called Decans. Each sign comprises 30 degrees (one twelfth of a circle) and each Decan contains ten degrees—in other words, one third of a sign. Those who were born under the first Decan of any sign are likely to be pretty typical of that sign, but those born under the second or third Decan will display some characteristics that are different because they have been "borrowed" from elsewhere.

The system is based on the *elements* of fire, earth, air and water. The first Decan of each sign repeats the sign itself, while the second Decan belongs to the next sign around the zodiac that shares the same *element*, and the third Decan comes under the last sign in that *element*.

List of the Signs and Their Elements

Fire Group:	Aries	Leo	Sagittarius
Earth Group:	Taurus	Virgo	Capricorn
Air Group:	Gemini	Libra	Aquarius
Water Group:	Cancer	Scorpio	Pisces

Examples

If your sign happens to be the first in a group (Aries, Taurus, Gemini or Cancer), the Decans fall into place as shown in the list. If your sign is in the middle or the end of one of the elemental groups, you just keep going round the system. Here are some examples:

» Aquarius is an air sign; its first Decan is Aquarius, the second is Gemini and the third is Libra.

» Scorpio is a water sign; its first Decan is Scorpio, the second is Pisces and the third is Cancer.

This theory is all very well, but a non-astrologer has no idea of which Decan he falls into, so the following Decan Calendar gives the approximate dates for all the signs and their Decans.

The calendar chart is pretty accurate, but the Sun doesn't always change sign or Decan on the same day each year, and only a full personal chart can give you total accuracy. We suggest that, if you happen to fall on the "cusp" of two signs or two Decans, that you read both to see which fits. You will spot the right one because the Decan system works so well.

Once you have found your Decan, turn to the chapter on that sign and read it as though it were your Sun sign. You will be surprised how much information it adds and how well it fits.

THE DECAN CALENDAR

ARIES

1st Decan: Aries	2nd Decan: Leo	3rd Decan: Sagittarius
March 21 - March 30	March 31 - April 9	April 10 - April 19

TAURUS

1st Decan: Taurus	2nd Decan: Virgo	3rd Decan: Capricorn
April 20 - April 29	April 30 - May 9	May 10 - May 20

GEMINI

1st Decan: Gemini	2nd Decan: Libra	3rd Decan: Aquarius
May 21 - May 30	May 31 - June 10	June 11 - June 20

CANCER

1st Decan: Cancer	2nd Decan: Scorpio	3rd Decan: Pisces
June 21 - July 1	July 2 - July 11	July 12 - July 21

LEO

1st Decan Leo	2nd Decan Sagittarius	3rd Decan Aries
July 23 - August 1	August 2 - August 11	August 12 - August 21

VIRGO

1st Decan: Virgo	2nd Decan: Capricorn	3rd Decan: Taurus
August 23 - Sept 1	Sept 2 - Sept 11	August 12 - August 21

THE DECAN CALENDAR

LIBRA

1st Decan: Libra	2nd Decan: Aquarius	3rd Decan: Gemini
Sept 23 to Oct 2	Oct 3 to Oct 10	Oct 11 to Oct 22

SCORPIO

1st Decan: Scorpio	2nd Decan: Pisces	3rd Decan: Cancer
Oct 23 to Nov 1	Nov 2 to Nov 11	Nov 12 to Nov 21

SAGITTARIUS

1st Decan: Sagittarius	2nd Decan: Aries	3rd Decan: Leo
Nov 22 to Dec 1	Dec 2 to Dec 11	Dec 12 to Dec 21

CAPRICORN

1st Decan: Capricorn	2nd Decan: Taurus	3rd Decan: Virgo
Dec 22 to Dec 31	Jan 1 to Jan 10	Jan 11 to Jan 20

AQUARIUS

1st Decan Aquarius	2nd Decan Gemini	3rd Decan Libra
Jan 21 to Jan 30	Jan 31 to Feb 8	Feb 9 to Feb 18

PISCES

1st Decan: Pisces	2nd Decan: Cancer	3rd Decan: Scorpio
Feb 19 to Feb 29	Mar 1 to Mar 10	Mar 11 to Mar 20

14

Your Best and Worst Time of Year

Use this chart from time to time when you need to check out a particular time of year. Two stars signify your best periods, while one star suggests a reasonable time. A zero shows a potentially troublesome period.

	ARI	TAU	GEM	CAN	LEO	VIR	LIB	SCO	SAG	CAP	AQU	PIS
ARI	**	*	**	O	**	*	O	*	**	O	**	*
TAU	*	**	*	**	O	**	*	O	*	**	O	**
GEM	**	*	**	*	**	O	**	*	O	*	**	O
CAN	O	**	*	**	*	**	O	**	*	O	*	**
LEO	**	O	**	*	**	*	**	O	**	*	O	*
VIR	*	**	O	**	*	**	*	**	O	**	*	O
LIB	O	*	**	O	**	*	**	*	**	O	**	*
SCO	*	O	*	**	O	**	*	**	*	**	O	**
SAG	**	*	O	*	**	O	**	*	**	*	**	O
CAP	O	**	*	O	*	**	O	**	*	**	*	**
AQU	**	O	**	*	O	*	**	O	**	*	**	*
PIS	*	**	O	**	*	O	*	**	O	**	*	**

15

Love and Compatibility

Although we cover your attitude to love and sex within the body of this book, we thought you might enjoy this quick guide to the signs that work best for you, in love and as friends.

YOUR SIGN	GREAT	GOOD	FAIR	AVOID
ARIES	Libra	Aquarius	Pisces	Virgo
TAURUS	Leo	Libra	Capricorn	Sagittarius
GEMINI	Aries	Virgo	Aquarius	Scorpio
CANCER	Capricorn	Taurus	Pisces	Sagittarius
LEO	Aquarius	Libra	Virgo	Aries
VIRGO	Cancer	Gemini	Pisces	Aries
LIBRA	Aries	Gemini	Aquarius	Pisces
SCORPIO	Leo	Cancer	Taurus	Virgo
SAGITTARIUS	Virgo	Capricorn	Pisces	Taurus
CAPRICORN	Scorpio	Cancer	Taurus	Leo
AQUARIUS	Aquarius	Sagittarius	Pisces	Cancer
PISCES	Pisces	Sagittarius	Aquarius	Libra

16

Compatibility at Work and Business

Some people are great to work with, while others rub you the wrong way. Check out the "compatibility at work" chart below to find your dream colleague or your bugbear.

YOUR SIGN	GREAT	GOOD	FAIR	AVOID
ARIES	Aquarius	Sagittarius	Virgo	Capricorn
TAURUS	Libra	Taurus	Pisces	Gemini
GEMINI	Aries	Leo	Libra	Pisces
CANCER	Taurus	Capricorn	Virgo	Scorpio
LEO	Scorpio	Virgo	Aquarius	Sagittarius
VIRGO	Gemini	Leo	Cancer	Aquarius
LIBRA	Taurus	Gemini	Aries	Capricorn
SCORPIO	Virgo	Capricorn	Aquarius	Taurus
SAGITTARIUS	Pisces	Aries	Leo	Cancer
CAPRICORN	Scorpio	Cancer	Taurus	Leo
AQUARIUS	Aries	Leo	Sagittarius	Pisces
PISCES	Virgo	Sagittarius	Leo	Scorpio

17

The Best Day and Hour for Your Sign

The Day Calendar

The days of the week are each ruled by one of the seven planets that are visible with the naked eye. Check out your sign's ruling planet, your sign, and its day to spot those that are likely to be lucky for you. You can even use the Decan system from the previous chapter to find a subsidiary lucky day if you like.

PLANET	SIGN	DAY
MARS	Aries	Tuesday
VENUS	Taurus	Friday
MERCURY	Gemini	Wednesday
MOON	Cancer	Monday
SUN	Leo	Sunday
MERCURY	Virgo	Wednesday
VENUS	Libra	Friday
MARS	Scorpio	Tuesday
JUPITER	Sagittarius	Thursday
SATURN	Capricorn	Saturday
SATURN	Aquarius	Saturday
JUPITER	Pisces	Thursday

The Hour Calendar

This is more complex, because the following table shows the days of the week along the top and every hour of the day in the left hand column. Track down and across to check which planet rules the particular hour on any day of the week. The information that follows will show you how the energies of each planet affect each hour. The Day Calendar on the previous page has already shown you which planet rules your sign, so you can now choose an hour that links with your planet to make a start on a particularly important matter. This kind of astrology is called *electional* astrology, because this way you get to *elect* the right time on the right day for a special event.

Note: In countries where British Summer Time or Daylight Saving is in operation during part of the year, deduct one hour during the affected summer months.

A Sun Hour
A joyful and successful hour

A Sun hour should be a happy and joyful one. Anything that you are considering setting out to do should have a great outcome if you start doing it during a Sun hour. A celebration that begins now should turn out to be a great success. If you are arranging a day or an evening in the company of someone you love, you will have a great

HOUR	SUN	MON	TUE	WED	THU	FRI	SAT
A.M.							
1	Sun	Moon	Mars	Mercury	Jupiter	Venus	Saturn
2	Venus	Saturn	Sun	Moon	Mars	Mercury	Jupiter
3	Mercury	Jupiter	Venus	Saturn	Sun	Moon	Mars
4	Moon	Mars	Mercury	Jupiter	Venus	Saturn	Sun
5	Saturn	Sun	Moon	Mars	Mercury	Jupiter	Venus
6	Jupiter	Venus	Saturn	Sun	Moon	Mars	Mercury
7	Mars	Mercury	Jupiter	Venus	Saturn	Sun	Moon
8	Sun	Moon	Mars	Mercury	Jupiter	Venus	Saturn
9	Venus	Saturn	Sun	Moon	Mars	Mercury	Jupiter
10	Mercury	Jupiter	Venus	Saturn	Sun	Moon	Mars
11	Moon	Mars	Mercury	Jupiter	Venus	Saturn	Sun
12	Saturn	Sun	Moon	Mars	Mercury	Jupiter	Venus

P.M.	SUN	MON	TUE	WED	THU	FRI	SAT
13	Jupiter	Venus	Saturn	Sun	Moon	Mars	Mercury
14	Mars	Mercury	Jupiter	Venus	Saturn	Sun	Moon
15	Sun	Moon	Mars	Mercury	Jupiter	Venus	Saturn
16	Venus	Saturn	Sun	Moon	Mars	Mercury	Jupiter
17	Mercury	Jupiter	Venus	Saturn	Sun	Moon	Mars
18	Moon	Mars	Mercury	Jupiter	Venus	Saturn	Sun
19	Saturn	Sun	Moon	Mars	Mercury	Jupiter	Venus
20	Jupiter	Venus	Saturn	Sun	Moon	Mars	Mercury
21	Mars	Mercury	Jupiter	Venus	Saturn	Sun	Moon
22	Sun	Moon	Mars	Mercury	Jupiter	Venus	Saturn
23	Venus	Saturn	Sun	Moon	Mars	Mercury	Jupiter
24	Mercury	Jupiter	Venus	Saturn	Sun	Moon	Mars

time. This is a good hour in which to set off for a holiday or to treat yourself to something that you fancy. It is even a great time to make love.

Anything to do with children or young people will go well if started at this time, and even if you only spend time kicking a ball around with your children, you will thoroughly enjoy yourself. This is a great hour for success in business or in a social setting, and if you need to be the center of attention for some reason, there couldn't be a better time. The Sun's association with gold and jewelry makes this a terrific hour in which to buy a ring or any other sparkly token of love for yourself or for your partner. Business matters should be also successful during this phase. Remember that the Sun god, Apollo, loved music. Therefore, if you want to play music, go to a musical event, or even to put on your favorite CD and relax for a while, this is a wonderful time for it. If you can do something that looks like being fun—even a game of Monopoly with the children—do it now.

A Moon Hour
An hour of sensitive feelings

There is good news and bad news connected to the Moon hour, because this can be one of those times when your emotions will burst through whatever has been keeping them in check. There are occasions when you can put up with almost anything, but this is not one of them. Things that usually pass you by almost unnoticed will get you down now. If there happens to be a Full Moon or an eclipse occurring on this day, you will suffer from a form of premenstrual tension—and this will be the case even if you are too old for it or if you are a man!

On the other hand, this is a great hour for home and family concerns. Anything from a family gathering to talking around the dining table with your loved ones or simply relaxing in front of the television with your nearest and dearest will be great now. Moving, decorating, or refurbishing your home or anything else of that nature will go well if it is started during a Moon hour. If you want to contact older family members or spend time with them, there couldn't be a better hour. You may feel restless during this time, so try to arrange a trip out somewhere rather than getting down to work or doing chores.

Sometimes the Moon acts as a trigger to events, so if you are waiting for something to happen, it should happen now. The influence of the Moon could make you quite perceptive and even psychic for a while.

A Mars Hour
An active hour

Mars is the action planet, so if there is something you need to do that requires action and activity, this is the time to go for it. There are a whole host of possible scenarios here but some ideas might include doing a tough, dirty, or heavy job either at work or home or perhaps working on the car. If you need to make a mental or physical effort at work for any purpose, get started on it during a Mars hour.

If you need to state your case or to put your foot down this could be the time to do so, but remember that Mars was the Roman god of war, so stand up for yourself but don't take things to the point where you start a real feud. Dealings with men will go well, and this applies to business matters or calling a builder or a workman to do something in your house. Passion in all its forms comes to the fore now, so lovemaking or passionate feelings will be reciprocated. If you are passionate about sports, you will be more energetic and competitive than usual, and you could end up the winner in any game in which you participate during this hour.

Even if you have a passion for something as innocuous as stamp collecting, you will find what you want and get where you want to be if you make the effort now. On a less pleasant note, you could find yourself at the dentist or undergoing some other kind of minor surgical procedure.

A Mercury Hour
A busy time with much contact with others

Mercury was the messenger of the Roman gods, and he often had to do the dirty work for Jupiter and Apollo. You can expect to make a few phone calls and deal with correspondence during this hour, but this doesn't mean that you will be expected to have to do someone's dirty work. It is simply a case of having to make contact with people and to communicate. You won't get much peace and quiet now, but you will manage to get a lot done.

There may be contact with brothers, sisters, and neighbors at this time, and if you need help or cooperation from them, this is a good time to ask for it. Mercury rules short journeys, so shoping trips or errands of any kind will go well now. If you need to get a vehicle fixed, this is a good time to arrange it.

Activities with young people and even indulging in gentle sport or other amusing activity will be good for you. You may be a bit rushed for a while, but you shouldn't be unhappy.

A Jupiter Hour
A time to expand your horizons

Jupiter was the king of the ancient gods and he could bring good or bad luck depending upon his mood. As far as an hourly reading is concerned, there are a whole host of things that are worth doing during this period. Jupiter rules the expansion of horizons, so you could book a trip or even arrange to travel at this time—especially a long-distance trip. Business that involves overseas customers or even dealing with foreigners in your own land will be successful during this hour. If you have any legal or official matters to cope with, this is a good time for them.

Jupiter rules education, so it's a good time to open your books and get down to studying, if this is applicable. Even if you only need to study how some new household appliance or computer program works, this is a good time to get your head around it. Jupiter rules belief and by extension religion, philosophy, and spirituality, so if you intend to go to a church meeting, a spiritualist event, a psychic event, or even to sit and think about what moves you, this is the hour for it.

Some see Jupiter as a lucky planet, and it is true that it is associated with gambling, especially horseracing. Therefore, if you intend to put a little wager on a horse or try your luck with the lottery, this is as good an hour as any for it. If the lottery is drawn during one of your Jupiter hours, this is even more likely to bring you luck.

Sometimes Jupiter will bring a breakthrough in business, but it can also bring setbacks. These, however, are usually followed by an improvement in circumstances or changes that need to be made.

A Venus Hour
A time for love, pleasure, and self-indulgence

Venus is the Roman goddess of love, so it is easy to see what this hour is all about! If you are planning a romantic meeting with a lover or a potential mate, this is the time for it. Romantic evenings indoors are equally well starred. Obviously this is a good hour in which to get engaged or married, but it is an equally good time in which to start a business or some other moneymaking enterprise. If you want to buy something special for the home, try to do it during this hour, and if what you are considering buying is good to look at, so much the better.

Practical jobs of a creative nature will go well during this hour, so if you are into gardening, cooking, or making attractive objects of any kind, this is the time in which to do it. Farming, working the land, or even buying stock for a farm should all go well if started at this hour. Money can be made from projects that are started now, especially if there is someone else who is involved—although it would be wise to check out the data for the other person as well as your own.

A Saturn Hour
A time for work and for sorting out details

Saturn can be a hard taskmaster, so this is the best hour for getting difficult jobs done and dusted. If you need to talk to a boss or to someone in a position of authority, try to schedule it for a Saturn hour.

Parents and older people are more likely to be helpful to you at this time, although you will have to put yourself out or make an effort to contact them. This is a good hour in which to start a long-term project, to put down roots, or to try to achieve stability in any sphere of your life.

Index